International Journal of Criminology

International Journal of Criminology

Vol. 5, No.1
Spring 2017

Editor-in-Chief
Alain Bauer

WESTPHALIA PRESS
An imprint of Policy Studies Organization

International Journal of Criminology: Vol. 5, No. 1, Spring 2017

Westphalia Press
An imprint of Policy Studies Organization
1527 New Hampshire Ave., NW
Washington, D.C. 20036
info@ipsonet.org

ISBN-13: 978-1-63391-592-3
ISBN-10: 1-63391-592-1

Cover design by Jeffrey Barnes:
jbarnes.design

Daniel Gutierrez-Sandoval, Executive Director
PSO and Westphalia Press

Updated material and comments on this edition
can be found at the Westphalia Press website:
www.westphaliapress.org

International Journal of Criminology

Volume 5, Number 1 • Spring 2017

Contents

Editorial Board

Prologue: The Ironic Growth of a Subject

Dr. Paul J. Rich

This welcome and newest issue of the journal suggests just how much ground is surprisingly now encompassed by the expanding notion of criminology. The growth of a subject is not unique, and we readily admit there are of course other fields that remained relatively static in some periods and then grew again -- mineralogy, for example, lost out in the early twentieth century to expanding geological sciences and then bounced back by venturing into new areas such as atomic structure. It is a truism that knowledge is not fixed, and even Roman history and Greek archaeology change.

So perhaps we cannot be too surprised or startled by the new concerns that are becoming part of criminology. Cyber hacking is a good example, as it would have belonged in an H.G. Wells novel just a generation ago. Border control has become the shrillest of political issues. The internet has even brought new crimes to high school youth, as they circulate nude pictures resulting in suicides. All this promises to be just the start of what we are going to see in forthcoming offences and offenders in areas well beyond yesterday's imagination.

There is a certain irony to the idea that social deviance is growing so fast thanks to technology, but there it is. Not only do we need to study and understand all of this, but we need to include these aberrations in the academic curriculum. If we do not, we will be even more the victims than we already are, as the wily and devious bound ahead with identity theft, credit card manipulation, and ballot box tampering.

My friends, read and reflect.

Paul Rich
President, Policy Studies Organization

Indefensible Space
Terrorism: Securing Places or Protecting People?

Alain Bauer[A] and François Freynet[B]

No matter the period, there are as many different types of target for terrorist attacks as there are attacks themselves: schools, as in Kiryat Shmona in 1974, Beslan, and Toulouse; concert halls, as at the Bataclan or in Manchester; nightclubs, as in Bali, Istanbul, and Orlando; airports—Tel Aviv in 1972, Rome, Orly, Algiers, Glasgow, Madrid, Moscow, and Brussels; metro, bus and train stations—Bologna in 1980, Paris, London, Madrid, Moscow, Montreal, Saint Petersburg, and so on; bars and hotels—Jerusalem, Bombay, Delhi, Mogadishu, Bamako, Sousse, Kabul, Baghdad, Tel Aviv, Paris, and so on; or shopping streets and supermarkets, in Omagh, Barcelona, and London.

With each attack, we discover once again how difficult it is to protect these targets, and concentrate on essentially static defensive measures. These are necessary, but they are insufficient. In this age of Twitter, we spend much of our time rediscovering; to a large degree, we have lost our sense of perspective and of detailed analysis. Many lessons that seem new to us are simply ones we have forgotten.

As emergencies and threat levels steadily rise, managing time and flows of people assumes the same importance as traditional security measures that typically impede and obstruct such flows. A state of emergency cannot be sustained over an extended period. The very idea is a contradiction. It is certainly necessary to reassure people by sending them the right message. But this should not stop us at the same time from beginning to fundamentally alter some essential concepts, and from moving beyond one-off responses.

The Limits of Defensible Space

One of the major theoretical questions in public safety concerns what is termed "situational prevention." In the early 1970s, the urban planners Oscar Newman and Jane Jacobs developed the concept of "defensible space." The idea was to design urban spaces so as to discourage crime and keep people from feeling unsafe. Even at that late stage, no one had recognized just how far living conditions had deteriorated; a culture of denial, along with a devotion to open spaces and to tearing down barriers, had stopped the hard debate about safety from taking place.

[A] Professor of Criminology at CNAM Paris, New York, and Shanghai

[B] Consultant. Both are authors, with Christophe Soullez, of *Comment vivre au temps du terrorisme* (Paris: First, 2017).

Meanwhile, in the streets and in the cinema, it was the age of "legitimate self-defense." The real world and the world of urban planning no longer coincided.

Nonetheless, principles informing security measures in urban planning were drawn up. The separation between private and public space, the marking of different territories, height limits, new types of formal and informal surveillance, and the "natural" appropriation of space—all of these concepts derive from the work of Jacobs and Newman. The principles of situational prevention have largely guided the implementation of regulations in France, especially following law No. 95-73 of January 21, 1995 and Article L. 14-1 of the Urban Planning Code. Regulations that apply these principles are now being adapted to the emerging terrorist threat. Such regulations typically reinforce the defensible spaces in question: improving security at potential targets, using video surveillance to monitor access more closely, reinforcing buildings, etc.

But the notion of defensible space has lost some of its relevance. There are a number of reasons for this:

- **Methods for improving security** and discouraging attacks lose their effectiveness when scaled to meet the risks of attack from wartime weapons and methods. In times of peace, buildings and facilities are designed to withstand peacetime attacks.

- **Access control** makes sense only if spaces can be closed, and if a distinction can be drawn between the public inside and outside them—leaving the attackers on the outside, of course. But recent incidents have shown that attackers are, in many cases, already inside the space. In reality, checkpoints are only passages between two open spaces, and the same people are present both inside and outside. There remains the further problem of vast interconnecting spaces that resist any attempt to define particular spaces within them.

- **Means of identification**, particularly video surveillance, are crucial for post-event analyses, but play only a weak preventive role in modern terrorist attacks.

- **Extending deterrent measures** is ineffective against individuals whose intention is to die, and whose primary concern is solely that they might not injure or kill a sufficient number of people.

Finally, **natural surveillance**—that is, surveillance by citizens—only works when there is a clear framework aligning public action with individual situations. This is very rarely the case in the current situation. Indeed, the state's inability to regulate the threat level produces a degree of disengagement on the part of citizens. We must also acknowledge that there are members of the public who are sympathetic to terrorist causes.

The succession of terrorist acts by the Islamic State—a group that is in no way innovative, but which has for the first time made use of the complete range of methods and agents available to such groups—leads us to question something we had taken for granted, bringing an end to the theory of defensible space. The sooner we grasp this, the sooner we can develop tools of resistance, rather than mere resilience.

Toward a Logic of Indefensible Space

Accepting the idea of indefensible space leads us to a new logic. Security measures no longer concentrate on static means of protecting a space, but on dynamic methods of protecting those within it.

Shortening the Timeframe

When an attack is in progress, time is no longer an ally but part of the danger. The first objective of any security organization should be to limit the number of potential victims by shortening the initial attack time, and then to evacuate people from exits unaffected by the attack, removing as many targets as possible from the path of the attackers.

This new requirement forces us to rethink our whole system of security measures. Most spaces open to the public—event spaces and commercial, professional, leisure, and cultural spaces—have increased their security measures in the wake of the Paris attacks on November 13, 2015. But security personnel have not established procedures that are very different from those in force prior to the attacks. Their methods of intervention have not changed; most would hardly know what to do if they detected something more dangerous than nail scissors.

Even today, the bulk of security measures are concentrated on prevention, with a smaller focus on detection. If there is no supervisor at the screening points at the entrances to these sites, or if they lack means of communication, clear procedures, and rapid reinforcements, these measures will not effectively spread the alarm. (And, of course, if the guards are attacked, they will be unable to raise the alarm.) This increases response times and, in particular, increases the length of time taken to evacuate the site.

Redefining Security Checks

We must therefore redefine the ways in which individuals are checked. Checkpoints must be seen as a way to quickly detect suspicious or threatening behavior rather than preventing attackers from entering the site.

Security checkpoints should be thought of as secure points where one can confront potential attackers. Ideally, there should be forces capable of reacting immediately at each such point. Their location should be determined by the means of protection (concrete barriers, stone blocks, etc.) and of evacuation (side passages, emergency exits, etc.) immediately available nearby. The number of these should be increased. The important thing is to limit crowding in front of the checkpoint, even if it means reducing the number of checks. The large number of open entrances to the Stade de France functioned well in the period prior to November 13, but reducing their number after the attacks has only been confusing and dangerous for the crowds gathered in the open external space.

Introducing Random Checks

One cannot protect all open spaces—streets, for instance—all the time. And, if one cannot be present everywhere, one must work in a mobile, random way. Recent terrorist acts show a mixture of preparation and improvisation. Random checks can disrupt such acts far better than fixed checkpoints. This is particularly true in the preparatory phases of these attacks, but also in moments of improvisation where they meet opposition they had hoped to avoid. Such random checks must be reinforced with techniques for coordinated armed patrols, and must have a way of communicating any alerts. Using agents specially trained to pick out individuals improves the effectiveness of such methods. Despite common criticisms, random checks do not represent a security failure. They are a positive force, as long as they are conceived of as such, and as long as they are tied into a system of checkpoints.

Evacuations during Attacks

The logic that drives the actions of public security forces often resembles that of firefighters. The police must prevent criminal acts, whilst firefighters make every effort to save as many lives as possible. In the case of a terrorist attack, these two groups work together to evacuate as many people as possible quickly and safely. It is generally not possible in such contexts to contain the targeted groups, because:

- These spaces are not designed to offer protection to those inside them.

- The officers in charge of containing the crowd will themselves be tempted to escape.

- A panicked crowd must be able to evacuate. If not, loss of life is inevitable, as in the case of Heysel stadium.

- No-one who manages a private space is competent or able to make the decision to confine the public within a space that has come under threat—for instance, by closing its doors.

Individual Adaptations to Indefensible Spaces

Adapting individual behavior relies on awareness of the security systems in use in indefensible spaces. It is a matter of living with the terrorist threat, and recognizing that our living spaces are not, at present, defensible spaces. Everyone is responsible, in part, for their own safety.

The Active Citizen's Attention

Recognizing the concept of indefensible space should not make individuals feel unsafe, or make them fear an attack is inevitable. Instead, it should keep them alert in the face of possible incidents. Living with the threat of terrorism requires us to adapt how we behave in public spaces, even ones that seem safe. It is no longer possible to leave one's safety in the hands of security systems and professionals without taking some responsibility for it oneself. Without descending into paranoia, we must become more attentive to the environment.

This is a condition of survival.

Anticipating Possible Attacks

Beyond this attention to our environment, we must anticipate possible attacks, no matter where we are. Identify escape routes and emergency exits to the side or rear of the site, and use this knowledge when deciding where to situate yourself. Report anything unusual to a security guard. Cooperate with security measures and checks: the faster they are carried out, the more effective they are.

Reacting to an Attack

Official safety guidelines drawn up in France following the attacks of November 13, 2015 are, of course, full of good advice. In the first instance, running and hiding are crucial for survival. In a sense, what action we take afterwards is unimportant. Nonetheless, adapting to events is essential. Common sense says that one should try to get away from the source of the danger as quickly as possible—from the noise of shots or explosions or, in the case of more distant alarms, from the sound of shouting. In all cases, one must get out of the attackers' line of sight or fire by taking shelter behind something sturdy. It is better, then, to escape via side passages, and to use curved or zig-zagged routes. While panic is natural, the ability to continue observing and adapting to the situation is crucial for one's chance of survival.

Accepting the Situation

Finally, we must talk about acceptance of the event. Each attack brings its share of drama, of personal stories, of despair and hope. And each brings with it heroes who save lives, provide shelter, fight attackers, and avoid dozens of casualties.

The victims of terrorist attacks are thrown into a universe of violence to which they do not belong and for which they are typically unprepared. Some will go beyond the guidelines of caution and self-preservation, choosing instead to fight. This is part of the acceptance of terrorist acts. There is no question of evaluating such actions: dead or alive, heroes are those who help save lives by placing themselves in danger. There are no good choices in such situations. Potentially, all will lead to further danger. But what would have happened if the Thalys passengers had fled instead of fighting? How many lives were saved on the Promenade des Anglais by the man who drove his scooter under the truck, making the vehicle slow and swerve? How many survivors owe their life to the policeman who shot the Bataclan attackers?

Of course, none of us know how we would react if faced with such an event. Those who underwent such experiences did not know how they would react. The state cannot demand heroism; ultimately, it can suggest only escape and survival. None of the measures we have described can be based on these exceptional individual reactions. But living with terrorism also means accepting the intrusion of war into some moment of our peaceful lives, as was the case this weekend in London.

We have learned to be vigilant.

We have become resilient.

It's now up to us to choose to resist.

Alain BAUER
Professor of Criminology at CNAM Paris, New York, and Shanghai.

François FREYNET
Consultant

Islamic State: Unidentified Terrorist Object

Xavier Raufer[A]

Threats and Consequences

The media had been in a frenzy since 2014, as the green stain of the "Islamic State" spread out over the map of the Near East like a hideous cancer. Worse, the self-proclaimed "caliphate" was gaining more and more ground. Then, abruptly, the media message changed in summer 2016. The Islamic State was in serious trouble, close to being annihilated.

But the threat has not gone way. A change in organization, or management in business school parlance, shouldn't be confused with disappearance. The "caliphate" does seem to have been well and truly weakened, but the question is why? Is it because it is being defeated militarily, or is it because, more profoundly and subtly, it has played its part? A part assigned to it long ago by certain players—perhaps one could call them its puppeteers?

This is a complex matter that requires much closer examination. Let's begin by looking at the following reality: slowly and surely, the daily flood of information and the increasing manipulation of this data stream have robbed the defense and security apparatus of its vital ability to understand the nature of the enemy. Faced with the very real dangers of our times, this blindness even worries the ideologues of the American military colossus. A researcher for the U.S. Army War College stated that, "We are faced with a whirlwind of crime and war which doesn't fit any familiar model. It's so unlike our conception of the world it ends up by driving everyone crazy. The result is that our thinking is behind the times, as are our institutions and our laws."[1]

It is clear that what defines all the hostile elements that have appeared since the fall of the Berlin wall is that they are no longer self-explanatory. In Europe, from the religious conflicts of the sixteenth century up until the colonial wars, it was always easy to identify the enemy. For the French, depending on the issue or the period, it was the Catholics or the Protestants, the English or the Germans. But for the last 30 years, we have been deprived of this age-old familiarity; the only thing in common amongst the people who kill in the very heart of our capital cities is that they are anything but self-evident.

Faced with this unpleasant reality, the defense and security apparatus reacts by burying their heads in the sand. Ignoring the old adage "know your enemy," the institutions imagine they know the enemy and haven't bothered to carry out the

[A] CNAM Paris

[1] Ioan Grillo, *Gangster Warlords. Drug Dollars, Killing Fields and the New Politics of Latin America*, Bloomsbury (NY), 2016. The researcher referred to is Robert Bunker.

diagnosis.

But can one really predict human hostility? Can one imagine future confrontations and enemies? Well, yes, one can, and sometimes even well in advance. In 1938, Carl Schmitt described the global unrest of the future in the following terms: "A global war, largely asymmetric, lacking any kind of control or legal limitations, in which a great neo-imperial power doesn't so much deploy its forces against individual states as against groups of global partisans (Kosmospartisanen) that operate worldwide using the means and pursuing the objectives of a civil war."[2]

Thus, today, a body of "global partisans" called "Islamic State" (hereafter IS), "Islamic State in Iraq and the Levant," ISIS, ISIL, "Daesh,", or the "tafkiris."[3] has been wreaking havoc amidst a huge media din. In this article, I aim to show that, whilst we are fed with stories of their atrocities, of terrifying figures of its weapons stockpiles and the size of its "armies," and whilst we are informed daily of its victories or its defeats—we have not yet answered the main question: what is, at bottom, the "Islamic State"? What is its nature?

First of all, what do we understand by the "nature of IS"? To find out, it helps to compare it with Hezbollah. Hezbollah, the "party of God," is child's play to define: Lebanese Shia militia, designed as a paramilitary, occasionally terrorist, organization; equipped, trained, and directed by the special forces of the Islamic Republic of Iran. Three lines provide one with the essentials. By comparison, the indefinable IS is far from self-explanatory.

Nearly 30 Years of History

Let's remind ourselves that this is neither a fleeting phenomenon nor some fundamentalist shooting star. Quite the opposite in fact. Under a succession of different names, IS has, in fact, existed for nearly 30 years. We will see below that this longevity has had far-reaching strategic consequences, but first, a reminder of some dates:

In 1989, the predecessor of IS was founded in Jordan under the name of "Jund al-Sham" (Soldiers of the Levant) by Abu Musab al-Zarqawi, for an objective which remains unchanged today: to combat the enemies of Islam—whether they be secularists or nationalists (such as Saddam Hussein or el-Sisi) or most importantly Shia Muslims, who, for Zarqawi, are a kind of proto-Christian cult polluting Islam. Jund al-Sham vowed to restore a caliphate which, when God wishes (insh'Allah), will bring all the Muslims in the world together.

In 1999, in Herat in Afghanistan, Jund al-Sham became "Jamaat al-Tawhid Wal-Jihad" (Congregation of Monotheism and Jihad). In 2004, it was renamed in Iraq during American occupation, this time as "Al-Qaeda in Mesopotamia."

[2] Carl Schmitt, *Guerre discriminatoire et logique des grands espaces*, Krisis, 2011.

[3] De Takfir wa'l Hijra is an Egyptian terrorist group which advocates an extreme form of Salafism, according to which most Muslims have descended into apostasy and thus deserve death.

Zarqawi was killed in June 2006, and, in October, the Mujahedeen Shura Council in Iraq (Al-Qaeda in Mesopotamia and its local satellites) founded IS in Iraq.

In April 2013, IS in Iraq and some Syrian Salafi belonging to the "Front for the victory of the peoples of the Levant" (Jabhat al-Nosra al-Sham[4]) created the "Islamic State in Iraq and the Levant."

On June 29, 2014, Abu Bakr proclaimed the caliphate and became caliph and "commander of the believers." Winning over the allegiance of all the Sunni in the world needs an army so the name was shortened to IS thereafter. This, in brief, is the history of the current IS.

But under the surface, beyond the image that IS projects of itself—wild Salafism, the cult of violence, paranoia—there are highly curious and improbable phenomena. One example is as follows: for Salafi, led by Zarqawi, Shia Iran, and "Alawite" Syria are the strongholds of apostasy. And yet, IS and its leaders have long been welcome in those countries.

So what is this IS and what is the thinking underlying its actions? What influences is it subject to? Or, perhaps, who is its puppeteer? As there is no officially sanctioned mission statement for the group, let us proceed by seeking the answers to four questions:

- What do we know about the career trajectory of the leaders of the IS, starting with its founder Abu Musab al-Zarqawi?
- What exactly has IS done on the ground? Why? And with what results?
- According to the evidence, who associates with and really supports the IS?
- Which states in the region infiltrate and manipulate the terrorist groups, even (or above all) when they seem hostile to them?

Impossible to Define

Is IS a conventional "terrorist group"? The answer is no; no terrorist group in the present day or in the past has ever possessed more tanks than the French army. In addition, since IS has been active in Iraq, there have been fewer attacks than previously. So, IS successes on the ground in 2014–2015 were clearly of a military and not a terrorist nature.

What is more, IS is active in the Middle East, where the unwritten regional rule is that all terrorist bodies inevitably mutate (rapidly) into state terrorism. This has been the rule for 50 years and there is no known exception. One recalls the cases of Abu Nidal (Fatah—Revolutionary Council) backed by Syria and then Libya; Ahmed Jibril (PFLP—General Command) backed by Syria, and ASALA, backed

[4] The majority of the leadership and fighters of Jabhat al-Nosra al-Sham rejected the merger and remained faithful to Al-Qaeda.

also by Syria.

Hezbollah itself is proof of this, as Pierre Razoux demonstrates in "Iran-Iraq War,"[5] which reveals numerous terrorism-based "indirect strategies." In 1985, King Fahd of Saudi Arabia made a goodwill gesture towards Iran and "as if by chance," in Beirut, Hezbollah released the Saudi consul, kidnapped there several months earlier by the Shia militia. Conversely, in the same year, Mikhail Gorbachev resisted Teheran's approaches and "in the absence of any reaction from the Kremlin, the Iranian leaders decided to switch up a gear, and on 30 September 1985, four Soviet diplomats were kidnapped in Beirut." Pierre Razoux adds that this was a strategy employed by all the leaders of Islamic Iran, whether they were in favor of opening up to the West or not. "For the former, the attacks against France were a means of forcing Paris to the negotiating table, whilst for the latter, they were aimed at punishing the "little Satan."[6]

Even Al-Qaeda hasn't been able to withstand the irresistible allure of state terrorism for long. It is now known that during his long stay in Abbottabad in Pakistan, Osama bin Laden lived under the close surveillance of the country's special services and was attended to by Major Amir A, a military doctor in active service, lodged for greater ease in the neighboring villa.[7] So is it really possible to believe that, by some miracle, IS has been able to dodge this unwritten rule for over 27 years.

Is IS a guerrilla army? Even less so; contrary to the tried and tested rules of "little war," IS doesn't retreat after an attack but digs in, controls territories, and confronts regular armies. To our knowledge, this strategy is unprecedented in the region.

IS, the strong arm of Sunni fundamentalism? In a matter not lacking in mysteries, this is a huge mystery. The supreme authority of Sunni Islam is al-Azhar, which is both the mosque of Cairo and a centrer of theology. Always prudent and considered, Al-Azhar condemns terrorism, whether Islamist or not, from a distance and with careful ambiguity. In 2010, the Secretary General of its Council deigned to certify the fatwa issued by Dr. Muhammad Tahir ul-Quadri (a Pakistani sufi), which limited itself to rejecting terrorism in general as anti-Islamic. But al-Azhar, or even one of its individual leaders, has never openly called a body of any sort "an apostate group," which would be tantamount to a death sentence. The response to Osama bin Laden and Al-Qaeda was silence, even after September 11, 2001.

In 2015, however, there was an abrupt volte-face: "Sheikh al-Azhar," the supreme leader of the institution, launched a verbal attack against the "oppressors and corrupt who combat God" and called to "crucify and dismember the ISIS terrorists." Why all of a sudden this violent condemnation of a type which al-Azhar

[5] Pierre Razoux, *The Iran-Iraq War 1980-1988*, Harvard Univeristy Press, 2015.

[6] Ibid.

[7] Abbottabad is the Pakistani equivalent of Saint-Cyr-Coëtquidan and is crawling with military personnel—not exactly the ideal location to lead a life in hiding. See "ISI Controlled Osama Bin Laden's Abbottabad Compound", *Press Trust of India*, 28 April 2016; and Seymour Hersch, *The Killing of Osama bin Laden*, London and New York, Verso, 2016.

had avoided ever since the foundation of IS?[8] There is convincing evidence that this was a response to the Saudi turnaround, which will be discussed below.

Lastly, it is worth noting that in "its" territories, its "caliphate," the administration adopted by the IS (control of the population, counter-espionage, etc.) has precious little which can be described as religious, as in Saudi Arabia, for example,[9] but in most matters is quite the opposite, modeled on the secular Ba'ath party dual system of surveillance and compartmentalization.

In their excellent book *Syrie: anatomie d'une guerre civile*, Gilles Dorronsoro and his co-authors have compiled numerous reports from the field, and they all describe this strange mixture of a fundamentalist or Salafist superstructure with the typical structure of "Arab Socialism": "Security practices inherited from the Ba'ath party…," "The presence of former Iraqi soldiers at the heart of the Islamic State…," "The same methods as during Saddam's dictatorship…," "The Ba'ath vision of the state plays a key role in understanding the organization of the caliphate…," "The Security Office is the equivalent of the former Iraqi régime's Intelligence Services," etc.[10]

The Strategic Context

Owing to its special role in the region, the United States is the country most concerned by IS. It is also definitely the country the world is looking to for a strategy, a counter-offensive. Yet, first in Iraq and Syria, and then in the IS territory, the United States has long struggled to come up with a workable concept.

In October 2011, when the American ambassador Robert Ford left Damascus, he was in the process of recruiting people for an (imminent post-Assad) government. At that time, American officials believed they had found the magic formula for régime change: the "Libyan model," according to which Washington supervised and provided the air attack, leaving operations on the ground and control of insurgents to the British and French special services.

But the East is complicated, and in December 2014, General Michael Nagata, commander of U.S. forces in the Middle East, confessed he "didn't even understand the idea" of IS. In September 2014, President Obama, the primary user of U.S. intelligence, called IS the "Al-Qaeda B team"—a major misjudgment.[11] The American intelligentsia hasn't done any better than the government: Between March and August 2015, the *New York Review of Books* and *The Atlantic*, two outstanding

---

[8] The pretext was a video of a Jordanian pilot being burned alive, but IS had committed worse atrocities many times before, and al-Azhar had not been moved to react.

[9] Inspired by the administration of Koranic schools, madrassas, etc.; or the *maktabi* model advocated by the Iranian Islamic revolutionary Ali Shariati. Xavier Raufer, *La Nébuleuse : le terrorisme du Moyen-Orient*, Fayard, 1987.

[10] Adam Baczko, Gilles Dorronsoro and Arthur Quesnay, *Syrie : anatomie d'une guerre civile*, CNRS EDITIONS, 2016.

[11] Literally "*Jayvee team of Al-Qaida.*" In sporting jargon: *Junior Varsity team* = B team.

journals, published three studies on IS.[12] Revealing a fascination with the finer detail, the articles are an example of "Salafism for dummies" and include the gory details of Jihadism, all the propaganda churned out to terrify, the return of slavery, foreign combatants, and so on.

On the other hand, there is no surprise about the nature and the aims of the group, which is quite unlike any other. What is this IS for? Who does it serve? Where does it really come from? What are its real intentions? These questions aren't even raised.

It is generally believed that the Gulf petro-monarchies, above all Saudi Arabia, support IS. Commentators have even suggested recently that Saudi Arabia is an "Islamic State" itself, having succeeded in founding a homeland, the Wahhabism of the Kingdom being no more than a variant of the Salafism conceived in the thirteenth century by Ibn Taymiyyah.[13] Up until 2014, this collusion was undeniable. In a secret internal note on December 30, 2009 (published by Wikileaks), Secretary of State Hillary Clinton condemned the Saudi financing of Sunni terrorism.[14] In fact, Riyadh's support for jihadis is logical: it's a question of combatting Iranian influence in the region and weakening, even toppling the Shia regime in Baghdad—anathema to the Wahhabis. But in 2014, the attitude of Riyadh changed. In March, it branded IS a terrorist body—doubtless as a result of American and European recriminations. Thereafter things deteriorated, especially following the death of King Abdullah, announced on January 23, 2015.

The change in Riyadh was rapidly picked up by IS, who took action on the Yemeni front. On December 6, 2015, a car bomb killed General Jaafar Saad, Governor of Aden and confidant of the (pro-Saudi) president, Abdrabbuh Mansur Hadi. And on December 25, Abu Bakr al Baghdadi broke his 7-month silence, denouncing Saudi Arabia as a traitor to Salafism and an ally of the "crusaders."

Since then, Saudi Arabia has cracked down on IS, with activists thrown into prison, networks dismantled, etc. The situation is particularly delicate for Riyadh as its theologians are divided on the matter—a tremendous risk for a theocracy. Some, including Sheikh Adel al-Kalbani (Imam of Mecca, the first African in the position) see IS as truly Salafist, but criticize its acts, not its doctrine; others, such as the sheikh Saad bin Nasser al-Shatri, a personal advisor to King Salman, describe IS as an "atheist gang, worse than the Jews and the Christians, who are fighting against God and his prophet, and whose members should be executed."

There is clearly a breach here between Riyadh and Mecca—which no Saudi power can tolerate. But did the Saudi turnaround come about willingly or was it

---

[12] "What is the Islamic State?", *The Atlantic*, March 2015; "Inside the Islamic State" and "The Mystery of ISIS", *New York Review of Books*, 9 June and 13 August 2015.

[13] Ultra-purist Salafist-Habali theologian of Kurdish origin, died in 1328 in prison in Damascus.

[14] "... Donors in Saudi Arabia constitute the most significant source of funding to Sunni terrorist groups worldwide... Saudi Arabia remains a critical financial support base for Al-Qaida, etc." (Memo—"Terrorist finance—action request for senior level engagement on terrorist finance", 30 December 2009, signed by Clinton).

brought about by force? Was Riyadh passed over or was control wrenched from it? These are issues which leave the question of the current collusions with IS wide open. In a region where all terrorist action is connected to states, who is now supporting IS? Let us now look at what is happening on the ground.

Surprising Actors, Strange Practices

"Abu Musab al-Zarqawi" was the founder and leader of IS, and is always praised as such in IS propaganda. His original name was Ahmad Fadeel Nazal al-Khalayleh and he was born in 1966 to a clan of the same name belonging to the Bani Hassan Bedouin tribe. When he became a jihadi, he adopted the nom de guerre "Abu Musab" in homage to his symbolic mentor and model, Musab bin Umair, companion of the Prophet, and "al-Zarqawi" from the Jordanian city of Zarqa where he was born. Al-Zarqawi is not a Salafist knight in shining armor, rather a dysfunctional Lee Harvey Oswald type: a video store assistant from provincial Jordan, a tattooed and alcoholic thug. He was imprisoned in the 1980s for drug addiction and sexual assault, and his family sent him for detoxification (through purification and prayer) to the al-Hussein ben Ali Salafist mosque in Amman. The success of the treatment exceeded his family's wildest hopes, as around 1988 the young Ahmad Fadeel founded the jihadi group Jund al-Sham, a murderous micro-sect. Zarqawi then left for Afghanistan (after the end of the anti-Soviet jihad). He was based in Hayatabad, near Peshawar, on the Pakistan-Afghanistan frontier, then in Khost in Afghanistan. He returned to Jordan in 1992 where, known as "The Afghan," he was closely monitored by the General Intelligence Directorate (GID). In March 1994, he was arrested with a stockpile of arms in his possession and sentenced to 15 years in prison, but then released in March 1999 under an amnesty following the death of King Hussein and the accession of the new king.

By then notorious as an *agent provocateur* and a paid killer, Abu Musab al-Zarqawi returned to Afghanistan with his followers. On his arrival, he was based near Kabul, in a sector controlled by Emir Gulbuddin Hekmatyar, a leader of the Pashtun tribal-Islamist Hezb-i-Islami party, his protector at that time.[15] In the year 2000, Zarqawi established himself in Herat, a town on the frontier with Iran teeming with agents of all kinds, and trained for terrorism with his gang.

Then followed the September 11, 2001 attacks, and on October 8, the United States began its purge of the Taliban and other terrorists. As a result of the offensive, foreign mujahidin fled to Pakistan. Not al-Zarqawi, who took refuge with 300 of his men…in Iran (for Salafis, the country of the "apostate Shia"). He lived there until spring 2002, under the continuing protection of Gulbuddin Hekmatyar.

[15] The ferocious Sunni former Afghan Prime Minister, G. Hekmatyar fled Kabul on the arrival of the Taliban in September 1996 and took refuge in Iran between 1997 and 2002, then returned discreetly to Afghanistan. Since then, his public statements have betrayed his pro-Iranian sympathies. In June 2006 (Associated Press – Peshawar) he paid tribute to Abu Musab al-Zarqawi, who had just been killed, and made an appeal to drive the Americans out of Afghanistan and Iraq.

In Iran, he was spotted in Zahedan, Isfahan, and Teheran. There is also mention by deserters of a training camp near Mehran. At the time, the Jordanian GID discovered that the "special operations" branch of the Guardians of the Iranian Revolution, the pasdaran al-Quds division, was providing him with arms, uniforms, and equipment.

Was this his personal initiative? Was the group commanded by Hekmatyar or by Iran? Zarqawi then took his first steps in international terrorism. In April 2002, the German special services dismantled one of his cells which was preparing anti-Jewish attacks. The German media published very specific information: pseudonyms, addresses, and phone and fax numbers. Faced with the outcry from Berlin, the Iranian authorities arrested Zarqawi and his accomplices. Evacuated to Syria and then to the Iraq-–Iran Kurdish border, they waited there for the American invasion. This stay in Syria is noteworthy, hosted by (for Salafis) heretic "Alawites," worse even than the Shia. Who was sheltering them? Why? In exchange for what? To this day, this mismatch has raised remarkably little interest.

From Decline to a Rapid Escalation of Power

Absent from any analysis of IS is one glaring incongruity. Abu Bakr "al-Baghdadi" (native of Baghdad) is not the first IS emir to use this nom de guerre. The previous one was called Abu Omar al-Baghdadi and was the first leader of a body then called "Islamic State of Iraq," officially created in October 2006 by Zarqawi's successor.[16]

Hamid Dawud Mohamed Khalil al-Zawi, known as "Abu Omar al-Baghdadi", (1947–2010), was a general in Saddam Hussein's famously secular police force—a curious background for a Salafist emir. Yet when he was killed near Tikrit in June 2010, the Iraqi press (which knows what it is talking about…) unanimously called "Islamic State of Iraq" a "small group." The same month, general Stanley McChrystal, American Joint Special Operations Commander in Iraq, noted that IS was in its death throes; its general staff had lost 34 of its 42 members and it was cut off from its Al-Qaeda power base, holed up in the mountains of the Pakistan–Afghan border.

Yet 3 years later (April 2013), this haphazardly armed bloodthirsty gang had morphed into Dawla al-Islamiyya fi'il Iraq wa'l Sham (IS in Iraq and the Levant). Between January 2014 (the capture of Fallujah) and June 2014 (when it entered Mosul), this "state," with its hundreds of armored vehicles taken from the fleeing Iraqi army, conquered the northern third of Iraq—over 150,000 km^2. According to military experts, this formerly "small group," cut off from Al-Qaeda, was "capable

[16] When Zarqawi was killed in Baqouba on 7 June 2006 by an American strike, Abu Ayub al-Masri, known as "Abu Hamza al-Muhajir, close to Zarqawi since 2003, assumed leadership of Al-Qaedxa in Iraq. In order to localize the uprising, in October 2006, he created Islamic State in Iraq, which brought together local guerilla groups and entrusted the emirate to Abu Omar al-Baghdadi. Both men were killed in a military operation close to Tikrit on 18 April 2010.

of encircling or isolating enemy units, sabotaging general staffs and enemy supply lines." It could "mount coordinated and simultaneous attacks" and its anti-aircraft capabilities were "serious" (helicopters downed). The little group even had drones and river gunboats. Its chains of command were effective, like its commando units and its intelligence (infiltration, recruitment, penetrations, murders, and attacks). It also had enormous stockpiles of weapons and munitions.

One should note that the United States, despite its vast resources, has invariably failed to construct anything like credible national armies... So how can this miracle be explained? How can one account for this sudden mutation of a small group into an army of conquest?

<u>Who is in Command?</u>

The conquest of northern Iraq in the first 6 months of 2014 stunned the world. The previously "small" group had undergone a mutation without anybody noticing—except those pulling the strings, and they certainly weren't going to boast about it. The United States, the Europeans, and the states in the Arab Peninsula and the Gulf, though directly threatened, hadn't seen it coming.

Subsequently, the powers active in the region did what they could to find out more about this mutant. Their efforts did finally produce a picture of IS, which was vague, but was nevertheless useful. Yet this picture differed so much from what the states concerned or the media thought they knew; and the story coming back from the terrain was so incredible that the main reaction was denial, everyone clinging to their old commonplaces, and nobody, at that time, incorporating the worrying discoveries into their strategies.

Reports coming from the ground were as follows: like all politico-military organizations, the IS apparatus had a pyramid structure, with the mujahidin at the base and the emirs at the tip. Yet, a painstaking analysis of the Who's Who of the real IS leaders (undertaken in Baghdad by the anti-IS coalition) revealed that at the head of this fanatic Sunni body, *there were no Islamists*.

Two points need to be made before continuing:

- Firstly, we know what a typical Islamist emir (warlord) looks like: he will have spent years fighting wars on jihadist fronts, in Afghanistan, in Somalia, and elsewhere; his exploits and his preaching will have been circulated on the Internet, in videos, and in forums, etc. If he is now middle-aged, his childhood exploits, his commitment, his conversion to the holy war, his entire hagiography will be clear to see: his youth in sin, the conversion, joining the jihad—all in preparation for his final martyr's death.
- Secondly, even if they were still incapable of predicting events, the immense electronic apparatus deployed in the Middle East was able to put together a trustworthy organigram of the IS military machine

within several months. It was possible to see the chains of command; the information that came up from the bases and the information that went down again made it possible to establish the pyramid referred to above.

Yet, the combination of these bodies of information indicates that the IS leadership is the prerogative of former officers of the Iraqi army and cadres from the Ba'ath party. More than 150 of Saddam Hussein's officers have been identified as IS personnel, in charge of intelligence, arsenals, and "special programs" (chemical weapons, etc.).

It should also be pointed out that, influenced by the origins of the "socialist" Ba'ath party, Saddam Hussein's army and party were paranoid bureaucracies bogged down in red tape; they kept thick dossiers on their personnel, Stasi-style, most of which survived the spring 2003 war.

The archives mined by the official experts have delivered up the following information: at the head of IS, the military leaders, or chiefs of intelligence and other technical functions (logistics, etc.), all come from the Iraqi army or from the Ba'ath party; their files reveal that before joining IS, they were secular or agnostic, living Western lives. On photos, their wives are bare-headed. Many of them were close to Uday, one of Saddam's two sons. In fact, their functions in the army and the party were such that if the painstaking controls they were constantly subjected to had revealed, not that they were Salafi but simply practicing Sunni, they wouldn't have survived long in their posts.

Between the defeat in 2003 and 2009, these members of the military resistance saw the inside of the prisons and camps of the American occupying forces: Abu Ghraib, Camp Bucca[17], and the little-known but key Tasfirat prison in Tikrit.[18] There they approached the Al-Qaeda fundamentalists who, until then, they had fought against or avoided like the plague. But in the Middle East, more than anywhere, the enemy of my enemy very easily becomes my friend.

Since 2014, the IS has been run by Ba'ath party cadres or Saddam's officers. Have they all seen the light, in some miraculous, collective conversion? Or are they mercenaries, previously bought by the dollars of the petro-monarchies and now... we'll deal with this key issue below. As it would be too long (and tedious) to name them all, here are some of the most well-known:

Waleed Jassem al-Alwani, known as "Abu Ahmad," Iraqi ex-officer, a member of the IS military council (majlis al-Askari) (probably killed in an air strike at the end of 2014).

Fadel Ahmed Abdullah Al-Hiyali, known as "Abu Muslim al-Turkmani"

---

[17] Military camp near the Iraqi town of Umm Qasr. The American occupying army maintained a (one hopes, unintended) "terrorist incubator" for years there.

[18] In September 2012, a sophisticated attack by what was then known as Al Qaeda in Iraq freed about a hundred rebels held at the prison. On the foundation of Islamic State seven months later, a number of them would become part of the structure.

or "Abu Mutazz al-Quraishi," member of the military council, officer in the special forces of the Iraqi army, and colonel of Saddam's military.[19]

Najem Fadel Adnan Ismaïl known as "Abu Abderrahman al-Bilawi," from the huge Bedouin tribe of the Dulaïmi, officer in Saddam's presidential guard; in July 2013, he escaped from Abu Ghraib, reached the military council, and died in June 2014 outside Mosul.

Adnan Latif Hamid al-Sweidawi known as "Abu Abdul Salem" and also "Abu Ayman al-Iraqi," colonel in Saddam's army, member of military council (killed in 2014).

And also "**Abu Ali al-Anbari**," formerly major general in Saddam's army, chief of military operations in Syria; **Taher Tawfiq al-Ani**, former Iraqi colonel[20], and many more.

Amongst the general staff and administration, where are the good, old-fashioned Islamists? Nowhere. Strange for a fundamentalist Sunni caliphate.

What Exactly Did IS Do in Iraq?

Let us now take a look at what IS did in Iraq, then in Syria, and the real consequences of their actions.

First one should remember that the Iraqi Shia remained largely faithful to Saddam during the Iraq–Iran war. Despite their emotional connection and reverence for Iranian Shi'ism and its holy places, they take objection to any "fraternal aid" coming from Teheran, which too often resembles the Soviet Union's help to Poland during the Cold War. When the supreme authority of Iraqi Shia, Ayatollah Mohammed Baqir al-Hakim, head of the Supreme Council of the Islamic Revolution in Iraq, returned from exile in Iran to the Iraqi holy city Nadjaf, he was expected to be fiercely opposed to American occupation, but he turned out to be conciliatory, ready even to engage in limited cooperation with the occupiers.

Let us now look at the actions of Zarqawi, who arrived in Iraq (via Kurdistan) at the beginning of 2003. The invasion of the country was completed on April 9 of the same year and on May 1, beneath the self-satisfied banner "Mission accomplished" on the Abraham Lincoln aircraft carrier, president George W. Bush stated: "Our forces and those of our allies have prevailed in Iraq." 111 days later, Zarqawi struck: on August 19, 2003 at 17:30, a booby-trapped truck destroyed the UN headquarters in Baghdad, killing 22 people, including the UN special envoy Sergio Vieira de Mello. The explosion was heard 20 kilometers away.

On August 7, as an omen of what was to come, a car-bomb had destroyed the Jordanian embassy, leaving 14 dead. These attacks stunned the intelligence services

---

[19] Supposedly killed in a drone attack near Mosul in northern Iraq on 18 August 2015 (according to Reuters, "The White House confirms the death of the Islamic State second in command", 21 August 2015).

[20] During the chaotic beginnings of the American occupation, Tawfiq al-Ani seized large quantities of arms and munitions, which were then handed over to IS.

active in Baghdad at the time, who had not seen them coming. The result was that Iraq froze, companies and international organizations fled or were paralyzed; reconstruction and a return to normal life became impossible. Iraq was plunged into chaos, a chaos which lasted until 2016.

On August 29, Zarqawi moved on to anti-Shia terrorism. In Nadjaf, a huge bomb was used to murder Mohammed Baqir al-Hakim and about a hundred of his co-religionists. The attack was claimed by Zarqawi, but experts read the signs of a special operation under jihadi cover. Worse still, on February 22, 2006, a huge attack laid waste to the Al-Askari shrine (the final resting place of Ali al Naqi and Hassan al-Askari, the 10th and 11th of the 12 Shia imams) in Samarra (destroying the dome, amongst other things).[21]

This final provocation by Zarqawi (after numerous others in 2004 and 2005) unleashed a Sunni-Shia civil war, leading to the murder of thousands of believers from both camps. Iraqi Shia, now obliged to beg for help and protection from Iran, were thrown into the arms of their "big brother." They had become vassals of Teheran. In Baghdad, the Iranian general Qasem Suleimani gained an important say in affairs and a rank akin to that of a proconsul.[22]

Between 2007 and 2009, the American *surge* was unleashed on Iraq, with 170,000 American soldiers in combat. It cost hundreds of billions of dollars a year, but was in vain. On December 18, 2011, the last U.S. army operational unit left Iraq.

What Exactly Has IS Done in Syria?

The Syrian civil war started in a low-key manner in Spring 2011, when the "Free Syrian Army" set out to conquer the "liberated areas." And then a branch of Al-Qaeda was established in Syria, under the name of Jabhat (Front) al-Nosra.

The *kataeb* of the IS entered Syria from the province of al-Anbar in Iraq at the end of 2011. One would suppose that they came to fight against their bête noire, the Alawite Bashar el-Assad, a faithful ally of Shia Iran, but in fact, as soon as they arrived in Syria, IS forces hurled themselves against the Free Syrian Army and Jabhat al-Nosra, and, under some specious religious pretext, occupied their positions, cut their leaders' throats, and massacred any militia refusing to swear allegiance to the caliphate. Compared to IS, the behavior of Bashar even looked acceptable. Hard on the heels of IS came general Suleimani and shortly afterwards, Shia militia, led by Hezbollah, arrived to bring succor to the Syrian regime. In turn, the Kurdish militia attacked IS, taking the pressure off Damascus.

In February 2014, Abou Khaled al-Suri, a Syrian leader of the coalition composed of Ahrar al-Cham and Jabhat al-Nosra, was killed in an IS suicide attack

---

[21] Built in 944 AD, the mosque received its golden dome in 1905, a gift from the then Shah of Iran. According to witnesses, the people who destroyed the mosque were wearing Iraqi ministry of the Interior uniforms.

[22] The greatly-feared general Suleimani commands the "Al-Quds force", a unit of pasdaran Iranians responsible for special operations in Syria, Lebanon, and Iraq.

in Aleppo. This bloody war between Islamist bodies caused thousands of deaths: focusing their efforts on "useful Syria" during this time, the Syrian army was keeping score. In August 2015, al-Nosra abandoned the north of Syria, following a wave of IS suicide attacks, causing 40 deaths. At the beginning of September, IS attacked the pro-American rebels on the outskirts of Damascus—and so it goes on.

From 2003 to this day, from Abu Musab al-Zarqawi to Abu Bakr al-Baghdadi, this is how the IS has been operating in Iraq and in Syria. But to what end?

Indirect Strategy: Key Strategy in the Middle East

Before considering the individual players, it is worthwhile looking at how the different armed groups active on the ground form, reform and break up, creating a kaleidoscope of mercenary groups. This dumbfounds European and American leaders today, but was actually long practiced in Europe, from the "free companies" of the Middle Ages to the *lansquenets* of the Wars of Religion.

In a warrior system resembling the football transfer market, shifty *kataeb* switch allegiance, camp, or activity (from guerrilla war to pillage or vice-versa) when they don't get what they want. In autumn 2015, for example, an IS *katiba* active in Mosul learned that their salary was being dropped from $400 a month to $200, and they immediately deserted and joined Jabhat al-Nosra, who was still being paid the "traditional" way—from the ample pockets of the petro-monarchies.

Trustworthy observers of these regional practices can confirm that transfers like this take place every week. And in IS itself, not to mention the more chaotic groups, numerous local commanders claim to have 250 fighters when they only have half as many, in order to pocket the fictional wages.

Phantom soldiers, disappearing armed groups, *kataeb* to the highest bidder, all this makes it very difficult for the European, particularly French, leaders to discriminate between "good" anti-Assad fighters (who are given arms) from "bad" Islamists from the IS (who are bombed), when these bands switch time and again from one camp to the other, simply for more money.

And it can be worse than that: at the end of 2015, Abu Fatima al-Tounsi, emir of Deir Ez-Zor, disappeared with all the mujahidins' pay, leaving them the following message on Twitter: "What state? What caliphate? What a bunch of idiots..."[23]

Teheran's Lengthy Experience

In June 2006, specific information regarding Iran's strategy in Iraq was revealed by *The Atlantic*. According to an intelligence officer in a country bordering Iraq, "The Iranians have a strategy: they want to control Iraq. They are therefore aiding Zarqawi tactically but not strategically. They give him arms, uniforms, and

[23] "ISIS falls prey to "ghost armies" who fight on both sides of the battleground", *Financial Times*, 21 December 2015.

military equipment, from the days of Ansar al-Islam.[24] And now (2006) they are letting Al-Qaeda operate there as well. Iran's war (in Iraq) is aimed at the United States; they will eliminate Zarqawi and his band when the Americans have left."[25]

In 2006, the American Joint Special Operations Command in Iraq also revealed that Al-Qaeda in Iraq and the Pasdaran special forces were cooperating in secret, the idea being to exacerbate the chaos in Iraq in order to drive out the Americans.

In September 2013, the *New Yorker* published a special report on General Suleimani, stating that, "At the beginning of the war in Iraq, Suleimani encouraged the head of intelligence for the Assad regime to facilitate the movement of Sunni extremists through Syria to fight the Americans. Al-Qaeda was also allowed a certain freedom in Iran. Kurdish leaders say that Suleimani's objective has always been to keep Iraq's parties divided and unstable, ensuring the country stayed weak."[26] As is evident, there are exceptions to the supposed unforgiveable enmity between Sunni and Shia.

All this Western intelligence has been confirmed by the leadership of IS itself. On May 2014, Abu Mohamed al-Adnani al-Shami, a founder and spokesman for IS, issued an audio-message containing a tirade aimed at "Sheikh Ayman al-Zawahiri, emir of Al-Qaeda." It was, in fact, a break with Al-Qaeda, entitled "Our apologies, emir of Al-Qaeda." Adnani reproached Zawahiri bitterly for having forced IS to spare Shia Iran "in order to protect its interests and its logistics in Iran. This makes Iran indebted to Al-Qaeda."[27]

The Damascus Virtuosi

What is described below would remain unknown were it not for Wikileaks, which at the end of November 2010 posted more than 250,000 State Department diplomatic dispatches.[28] On February 18, 2010, Daniel Benjamin, State Department Coordinator for Counterterrorism, met with Faisal Mekdad, the Syrian Deputy Foreign Minister, together with the Syrian ambassador to Washington.

Surprisingly, Ali Mamlouk, the discreet director general of the Syrian intelligence service, was also present. It is important to note that the presence of Ali Mamlouk at the meeting was unprecedented in Syria. He was there on the orders of Bashar al-Assad, who was seeking to develop a closer relationship with President

[24] First called Jund al-Islam, then Ansar al-Islam, the armed Arab-Kurdish group was active between 2000 and 2002 in Iraq-Iranian Kurdistan. Composed of Afghan jihadi veterans, the Salafist group was fighting against Sadam Hussein's Iraq—and for that reason were aided by Iran. In 2002, Zarqawi's Tawhid group was active within Ansar al-Islam. Subsequently, the survivors of the group joined Al-Qaeda in Iraq, and then Islamic State in Iraq.

[25] "The Short, Violent Life of Abu Musab al-Zarqawi", The Atlantic, July 2006.

[26] "The Shadow Commander", The New Yorker, 30 September 2013.

[27] https://pietervanostaeyen.wordpress.com/2014/05/12/new-audio-message-by-isis-shaykh-abu-muhammad-al-adnani-as-shami-apologies-amir-al-qaida.

[28] US Department of State Cf. study sources.

Obama. General Mamlouk extolled the counter-terrorist expertise of Syria, which had been fighting the Muslim Brotherhood for some 30 years. But Damascus has a different approach to Washington. "Normally," said Mamlouk, "we don't attack them, we don't kill them directly. We infiltrate them first ('a complex process,' stressed the general), and we don't act until the time is right."

Still bogged down in Iraq, would the United States put up with the infiltration of foreign soldiers? Washington should let Damascus get on with it, suggested Ali Mamlouk, as they knew a whole lot more about the takfiris. "We have wide experience. We know them. We are on home ground. Let us deal with it" to the benefit of both parties. "Of course," he concluded, "we would like to be taken off the list of states which sponsor terrorism and we also need spare parts for our aircraft… But these are modest requests."

In brief, help us to help you. This was a friendly proposal, certainly, but also a subliminal threat, as who can *really* say where infiltration finishes and manipulation begins? And what easier than to eliminate a danger that one has created oneself? The following spring, civil war broke out in Syria, the American ambassador left Damascus in October 2011, and it came to nothing. This does, however, provide a striking insight into Syrian, and by the by, Iranian, indirect strategy in the region.[29] What follows are some specific examples of Mamlouk's method.

- In September 2007, an American commando killed "Abu Muthanna al-Ansari," leader of the "Sinjar" organization, which takes its name from the Iraqi town in the province of Nineveh which neighbors Syria. During the operation, the commandos seized the (spring 2006 to summer 2007) archives of Abu Muthanna's Iraq–Syria operations. They turned out to be a treasure trove: detailed books of accounts, logistics, and administrative inventories, and personal files on 576 foreign jihadi travelling through to Iraq—212 of them on "suicide operations." All Al-Qaeda's "import-export" and "human resources" bureaucracy is recorded: infiltrations and exfiltrations, funding, smuggling, etc.[30] The documents show that, in the full knowledge of the Syrian special services, the following jihadi passed through the country: 237 Saudis, 111 Libyans, 46 Syrians, 44 Yemeni, 41 Algerians, 36 Moroccans, and 11 Jordanians.

- On October 20, 2008, in the Syrian frontier town of Abu Kamal, an American Joint Special Operation Command, which had come into the country from Iraq, killed "Abu Ghadiya," an Iraqi Al-Qaeda cadre.

---

[29] And the strategy has a long history: Hafez al-Assad, Bashar's father, was constantly engaged in this manner during the entire Lebanese Civil War (1975-1990).

[30] "*Treasury designates members of Abu Ghadiya's network facilitates flow of terrorists, weapons and money from Syria to al-Qaeda in Iraq*" (US Department of the Treasury, 28 February 2008).

Originally called Badran Turki Hisham al-Mazidih, this Iraqi from Mosul had run Al Qaeda's cross-border logistics operation since 2004. From Syria (which was supposedly tracking the jihadis), his logistics operation was supplying Zarqawi, and then his successor, Abu Ayub al-Masri, with money, arms, men, counterfeit papers, guides, and hideouts, etc. Yet here the document also revealed Abu Ghadiya's close links with Assef Shawkat, at that time leader of the Syrian military intelligence service and Bashar el-Assad's brother-in-law.

- And lastly, there is this recent and troubling report by Mohamed Qassim, a moderate opponent of the Damascus régime, and previously prosecutor in the Syrian town of Tadmur. In April 2015, this level-headed lawyer saw the Syrian army abandon the city, which shortly after was seized by IS. The aim of the withdrawal strategy was to bring IS into direct contact with the Jaish al-Islam (Army of Islam) rebels in the neighboring region of Qalamoun, so that IS could destroy them.

Who Is Pulling the Strings?

The IS is clearly a mercenary army. It is neither an uprising nor a guerilla army—least of all a terrorist group. But can one be a mercenary in one's own service? Of course not. And hence the fundamental question: who are they serving? Or, rather, as the region defies any simplistic analysis, who is able "to influence" this machine in its own interests and who is in a position to do so?

On this point, Saudi Arabia is now on the sidelines—or has had its *pitbull* stolen. And the other Gulf petro-monarchies are incapable of conducting such weighty, long-lasting, and complex operations. Who else is there in the region? Who might be responsible? Who would be in a position to do so? Because such indirect and bloody strategies are complex to mount, and even more complex to conduct with any degree of finesse.

One of the plausible candidates is the Islamic Republic of Iran. It certainly has a long and rich track record of terrorist indirect strategies:

- The Sunni Tunisian Fouad Ali Saleh was recruited and trained by the Iranian services for the 1985–1986 Paris attacks.

- During the 1990s, Ankara military intelligence created a Turkish Hezbollah, in reality a Kurdish gang in Turkey, in order to eliminate the personnel belonging to the Kurdistan Workers' Party (PKK). But then the Iranian special services gained control of this local Hezbollah and used it to kill dozens of government opponents in Teheran, in Turkey, and in surrounding countries. The affair caused quite a stir at the time; there were trials in Turkey and a number of publicly available documents exist on this ignominious affair.

Let us now look at the states in the Shiite arc, which stretches from Iran, through Iraq and Syria, through to Southern Lebanon. All of them clearly have dreams of putting Sunni extremism out of action. Some of them have considerable resources and skillful operators at their disposal, and have engaged in indirect strategies for many years. And for the leaders of the countries in this arc, the IS is a propaganda and communication gift: a media calamity…throat-slitting…butchers… rape of slaves…appalling destruction of heritage. What better to horrify the planet? And Muslims too. And once IS is eliminated, who would dare advocate Salafism in the decades to come?

Even if it meant discreetly embellishing Salafist-jihadist ideology, Mustafa Setmariam Nasar, an Al-Qaeda dissident called Abu Musab al-Suri ("the Syrian"), is the ideologue of neo-jihad, and has written a 'bible' on the subject in English, entitled "Call for worldwide Islamic resistance," which serves as the operational framework for IS operations abroad. But where did al-Suri write his work? According to a November 2016 article in the *New York Review of Books* by Ahmed Rashid entitled "Seeing the despair of jihad," he wrote it "in Iran, where he was a refugee at the time."

That is not all. The main character in the middle-eastern game is, of course, the United States. Its strategy was to pursue two goals in order to extricate itself from the disasters of the Bush years. In Syria, it sought to create a "modest" opposition to Bashar el-Assad, leading to regime change in Damascus. In Iraq, it sought to create a government which could make the Sunni-Shia religious war a thing of the past.

And who but IS has kicked these two projects, the mere mention of which now brings a smile to the face, well into touch? And what option has been left to the White House to avoid regional checkmate? It has little option but to follow Teheran's lead, the capital of the empire which invented the game of chess.

We know that in the Middle East, state terrorism has the intangible goal of appealing to the adversary of the moment to negotiate or to evolve. This type of terrorism is not designed to punish or to exact vengeance. So when an attack originates in the Middle East, any country which is a victim should ask itself very quickly: Whose toes have I trodden on by mistake? What blunder have I committed? What is the message? Who can explain it to me? Because these terrorist missives are never marked "return to sender." When you don't know where it comes from, the attack is so much more terrifying.

Is it not now time to dedicate our efforts to the work of deciphering the messages? Not in order to capitulate, of course, but in order to *understand.* A close scrutiny of the "influences" to which the succession of "Abus" at the head of IS are subject would probably be the best way to illuminate the present and throw light on the future of Islamist terrorism, in the Middle East of course, but above all, in Europe.

This is a quest which doesn't seem entirely futile.

Dossier - The New Habits of Imperialism
The Geopolitics of American Law: Recent News from the Foreign Front

Olivier de Maison Rouge[A]

"France does not know it, but we are at war with America. Yes, a permanent war, a vital war, an economic war, a war without death. . . apparently. Yes, they are very hard, the Americans, they are voracious, they want undivided power over the world. (. . .) It is an unknown war, a permanent war, a war apparently without death and yet a war to the death!" These words were said by François Mitterrand towards the end of his life.[1] Even before his reelection in 1988 he had predicted: "It is time, in fact, to address the situation. Consider the global economy: it is nothing but a battlefield where businesses are engaged in a war with no quarter. No prisoners are taken. Those who fall, die. (. . .) Attacks on enemy territory mean that to survive, you cannot stay where you are. The conquest of exterior markets protects the interior market (to export, to implant oneself in a foreign land). As for reliable allies, they are in short supply. Let us not forget that this war is a total, general war. (. . .) Relaxation is unforgivable. The fate of the nation is at stake."[2]

The President of the Republic deliberately chose hawkish language, no doubt because he felt it was the most appropriate way to express a reality that he had been aware of for a long time, and which has intensified since then.

The fall of the Soviet Bloc effectively allowed the United States to shape what George H. W. Bush called a "New World Order." The American Empire accordingly spread its ideal of "doux commerce," to use Montesquieu's famous phrase. The year 1991 was supposed to draw the curtain on the "short twentieth century"[3] with the victory of the so-called liberal world, a unipolar system covering the entirety of the globe. Its expansion was particularly clearly expressed in the Treaty of Marrakech that founded the World Trade Organization (WTO), signed on April 14, 1994. Almost all the world's nations are now members of the WTO. It was intended to be the sole international authority for economic and commercial (de)regulation, with a focus on free trade, and more generally, the free circulation of goods, people, services, and cash flows. More recently, the WTO appears to have reached the limits of it power with

[A] Lawyer and Doctor of Law. Most recent publication: "Le droit du renseignement. Renseignement d'Etat, renseignement économique" LexisNexis, 2016.

[1] Georges-Marc Benamou, Le dernier Mitterrand (Paris: Plon, 2007).

[2] François Mitterrand, "Lettre à tous les français, § La guerre économique mondiale" (letter addressed to the French people, April 6, 1988).

[3] Begun in 1914 with Europe's collective suicide that led to the consolidation of the USA's industrial and then financial power.

the Doha Development Cycle, which has stalled while its member states are unable to come to an agreement.

Meanwhile, a parallel reality was taking shape as the BRICS nations emerged onto the international stage. The paradigm shift from a unipolar to a multipolar world is changing power relations and strategies profoundly and, no doubt, permanently. The United States has had to imagine new scenarios.[4] For Pascal Boniface, Director of IRIS (the French Institute for International and Strategic Affairs), "the unipolar world was an illusion that took George Bush and the United States into the Iraq War, a fiasco that weakened American power. (. . .) The emergence of other powers led to the United States, and the Western world more generally, losing its monopoly on power. The excessive use of violence by the United States made American power more unpopular, and so less powerful."[5]

The dwindling of American power is clear. However, it is only a relative decline that by no means implies the USA's withdrawal from its traditional zones of influence, unless Donald Trump's stance deliberately increases the temptation of isolationism. The United States has up until now tried to maintain its dominance, or advantage, over Europe, and at the very least to weaken the old continent in order to establish its own position of power more firmly. It understands the need to be strongest when dealing with the weakest. This article will try to decipher the main driving forces behind its actions.

Extraterritoriality or the Ascendency of American Law

To paraphrase von Clausewitz, who stated that "war is the continuation of politics by other means," we suggest that "law is the continuation of economic warfare by other means." The United States sees itself as the bearer of a messianic, evangelical mission, and as such claims universal judicial competence. In this spirit, it has recently undertaken several initiatives aimed at extending its judicial hegemony even further, some of which are discussed below.

The Foreign Corrupt Practices Act (FCPA) is a federal law adopted in 1977 and intended to combat corruption in the business world. It can be enforced by the Department of Justice (DOJ), but also by the Federal Bureau of Investigation (FBI), the National Security Agency (NSA), or the Securities and Exchange Commission (SEC). The investigative resources available to these bodies are extremely wide-ranging. They can access any business-related information or documents they want, however confidential such information might be.[6] They are authorized to conduct interrogations with no lawyers present. Thanks to the generally broad approach taken

[4] *Le monde en 2030 vu par la CIA* (Paris: Editions des Equateurs, 2013).
[5] "Le monde occidental a perdu le monopole de la puissance." Interview with P. Boniface in *Libération*, April 5, 2016.
[6] For further information, see Olivier de Maison Rouge, "Procédure participative & discovery, faux amis ou vrais jumeaux de justice négociée?," Village de la Justice http://www.village-justice.com/articles/procedure-participative-discovery,19153.html (accessed April 18, 2017).

by the American tribunals, the FCPA can target a foreign company regardless of whether there is any link between it and the United States. The word "extraterritoriality" refers precisely to this phenomenon of the criminal law of a state, having been adopted by its national representatives, being used to wield power over an economic actor outside the borders of that state.

In the same spirit, the Sarbanes-Oxley Act (SOX), which came into force on July 30, 2002, is intended "to increase corporate responsibility, to make financial disclosures more reliable and to combat deviant and fraudulent behavior on the part of companies." SOX directly impacts foreign companies insofar as it applies to all companies listed on the New York Stock Exchange (NYSE). Numerous French and European companies are affected. SOX imposes heavy sanctions on French companies listed in the United States. If CEOs do not meet financial reporting requirements, they risk 20 years in jail and a fine of €5 million.[7]

The case involving BNP Paribas, which culminated in the French bank paying a record fine to the American administration,[8] is a good illustration of this assumption of the power to impose American laws. The justification for the fine was a transaction denominated in dollars connected to an investment in Iran, a country that the United States had placed under sanctions prohibiting any economic exchange. The only link to the United States was that the financial compensation had been processed through American accounts. No transactions were carried out on American soil.

It is important to emphasize that this case did not take the form of a legal proceeding before a tribunal with rules allowing for adversarial exchange, but rather of a dossier handled directly by an authority[9] to which BNP Paribas had no choice but to submit. It pleaded guilty to avoid a trial that would have been long and costly, and that could have had an even worse effect on its reputation.[10] Under pressure, it agreed to a financial deal: intimidation triumphed over the principle of open justice.

For the same reasons, and in a similar context, Crédit Agricole was fined $787 million as punishment for transactions carried out—and paid for in American currency—in Iran, Sudan, Myanmar, and Cuba between 2003 and 2008.[11] This amicable solution allowed the financial institution to retain its banking license and avoid any criminal sanctions. Negotiated justice of this type works in favor of the American treasury. The American authorities used the same embargo laws to order Peugeot to withdraw from Iranian territory in 2012, only to replace it with General

[7] Alexandre Moustafa, "Ces lois américaines qui font frémir les entreprises françaises," *Portail de l'IE* (November 21, 2015), http://portail-ie.fr/article/1308/Ces-lois-americaines-qui-font-fre-mir-les-entreprises-francaises (accessed April 18, 2017).

[8] Antoine Garapon and Pierre Servan-Schreiber, eds., *Deals de Justice, le marché américain de l'obéissance mondialisée* (Paris: PUF, 2013). See also Anne de Guigné and Pierre-Yves Dugua, "BNP Paribas tremble et implore la clémence des Américans," *Le Figaro*, May 13, 2014, or Mathilde Damgé, "La chambre de compensation, la clé de l'amende BNP," *Le Monde*, June 3, 2014.

[9] The Department of Justice (DOJ).

[10] The negotiated fine was raised to seven billion US dollars.

[11] Pierre-Yves Dugua, "Amende de près de 700 millions d'Euros pour le Crédit Agricole, *Le Figaro*, October 20, 2015.

Motors (although when the boycott was lifted, Peugeot had maintained its position and was able to come back even stronger with Citroën).

These examples show the Americans trying overtly, and not without brutality,[12] to use blackmail during trials (the outcomes of which are still effectively unknown) in order to control economic actors. Clearly, the United States has passed from soft law—the choice of economic and legal systems that are non-binding but derived from its model (OECD, WTO, and transnational treaties)—to hard law. Its aim is to enforce its own economic and commercial rules, backed up by a formidable and combative judicial system, in order to reduce competition for its own interests—even to the point of generating blatant distortions of competition. This asymmetrical war, in which the extraterritoriality of law has become the principal weapon, is a new conflict. The DOJ is its military arm. "Far from being an end in themselves, these sanctions have enabled the United States to preserve, or even develop, markets for their domestic companies by weakening their competitors under the guise of respect for the environment (BP, VW) or for democracy (PSA, BNP)."[13]

The Accusation of Corruption, Vice's Tribute to Virtue?

"Corruption is the cancer at the heart of so many problems we need to tackle in our world," announced David Cameron on May 10, 2016. It is impossible to disagree with the sentiment, even if the scale of the problem is arguable. The Americans, however, animated by the moralizing spirit inherited from their original messianic role—confident that the United States is justified in prohibiting and stigmatizing reprehensible activities, but not acknowledging that its economic violence is a blameworthy act in itself—have elevated corruption to the status of absolute evil.[14] This helps them oust competitors from, or at least destabilize, certain markets. In the process, local traditions and cultures are often disregarded or misinterpreted as being corrupt.

Corruption may have been commonplace for large contracts until a few years ago, and indeed several multinationals have been publicly condemned for it, but it has become significantly less widespread since then. And yet, rightly or wrongly, it is still not uncommon to see an American company discredit and/or stigmatize a competitor by insinuating that it engages in wrongdoing, even if the allegations are unfounded.

---

[12] During the Alstom case, senior executives' passports were confiscated while travelling in Asia. They were interrogated and placed in solitary confinement, with no legal guarantee, in violation of the rights of the defence. Jean-Michel Quatrepoint, ALSTOM scandale d'Etat (Paris: Fayard, 2015).

[13] Angéline Steinbach, "Sanctions américaines records: un moyen pour les Etats-Unis de controller leur environnement concurrentiel économique?," Portail de l'IE (October 27, 2015), https://portail-ie.fr/analysis/1293/sanctions-americaines-records-un-moyen-pour-les-etats-unis-de-controler-leur-environnement-concurrentiel-economique (accessed April 18, 2015).

[14] "Accusation de corruption, l'arme atomique," Intelligence Online 678. https://www.intelligenceonline.fr/renseignement-d-affaires/2012/12/12/accusation-de-corruption-l-arme-atomique,107936003-EVE (accessed April 18, 2017).

When the accusation of corruption becomes anathema and can be used to drive out competitors, the crime itself becomes a commercially attractive tool.

At a time when France is strengthening its anti-corruption legislation,[15] it is important to understand what corruption actually means in practice. To do so, we need to turn to the main NGO working in this area, Transparency International. It publishes a global corruption perception index (CPI) every year. The CPI measures a perception, and not an objective fact, something that has been picked up on by *Le Monde*.[16] Elsewhere, the Fondation Prometheus regularly highlights the fact that Transparency International is not an independent organization, which casts some doubt on the NGO's real motives.[17]

Transparency International understands corruption as follows:

> "Generally speaking as 'the abuse of entrusted power for private gain.' Corruption can be classified as grand, petty, and political, depending on the amounts of money lost and the sector where it occurs.
>
> Grand corruption consists of acts committed at a high level of government that distort policies or the central functioning of the state, enabling leaders to benefit at the expense of the public good.
>
> Petty corruption refers to everyday abuse of entrusted power by low- and mid-level public officials in their interactions with ordinary citizens, who often are trying to access basic goods or services in places like hospitals, schools, police departments and other agencies.
>
> Political corruption is a manipulation of policies, institutions and rules of procedure in the allocation of resources and financing by political decision makers, who abuse their position to sustain their power, status and wealth."[18]

In French law, Article 432-12 of the Penal Code defines corruption as:

---

[15] The law known as Sapin 2.

[16] Benjamin Bruel, "Comment mesure-t-on la corruption dans le monde?," *Le Monde* (May 13, 2016), http://www.lemonde.fr/les-decodeurs/article/2016/05/13/comment-mesure-t-on-la-corruption-dans-le-monde_4919107_4355770.html (accessed April 18, 2017).

[17] "Transparency International: une éthique à géométrie variable," last modified December 2012. http://www.fondation-prometheus.org/wsite/publications/a-la-une/transparency-international-une-%c3%a9thique-%c3%a0-g%c3%a9om%c3%a9trie-variable/ (accessed April 18, 2017).

[18] "FAQs on Corruption." https://www.transparency.org/whoweare/organisation/faqs_on_corruption/2/ (accessed April 18, 2017).

> "The direct or indirect request or acceptance, unlawfully and at any time, of offers, promises, donations, gifts or advantages of any type, by a person holding public authority or discharging a public service mission, or by a person holding a public electoral mandate, whether for his or any other person's benefit, where such advantage is requested or accepted:
>
> 1) as an inducement to carry out or abstain from carrying out, or as a reward for having carried out or abstained from carrying out, an act relating to his office, duty or mandate, or facilitated by his office, duty or mandate;
>
> 2) as an inducement to abuse, or as a reward for having abused, his real or alleged influence with a view to obtaining from any public body or authority any distinction, employment contract or any other favorable decision."

And again, under article 433-1 of the same Code:

> "Unlawfully proffering, at any time, directly or indirectly, any offer, promise, donation, gift or advantage, to a person holding public authority or discharging a public service mission, or holding a public electoral mandate:
>
> 1) to induce him to carry out or abstain from carrying out, or to reward him for having carried out or abstained from carrying out, an act pertaining to his office, duty or mandate, or facilitated by his office, duty or mandate;
>
> 2) to induce him to abuse, or to reward him for having abused, his real or alleged influence with a view to obtaining any distinction, employment, contract or any other favourable decision.
>
> The same penalties apply to yielding before a person holding public authority or discharging a public service mission, or holding a public electoral mandate who, unlawfully and at any time, solicits offers, promises, donations, gifts or advantages of any type, for himself or for any other person, as a reward for carrying out or abstaining from carrying out any act specified under 1), or for abusing his influence under the conditions specified under 2)."

Wikipedia (French version) suggests this definition: "Corruption is the perversion or misappropriation of a process or interaction involving one or several individuals with the aim, on the part of the corrupter, to gain specific advantages or prerogatives, and on the part of the corrupted, to gain a reward in exchange for his or her compliance. It generally results in the personal enrichment of the corrupted person or the corrupting organization (mafia gang, business, club, and so on). It is a practice that may be considered unlawful depending on the domain concerned (commerce, business, politics, etc.)."

However, it is important not to use these definitions to judge the traditional cultural practices found in some social systems as corrupt. Doing so would make such cultures liable to be sanctioned and could undermine ancestral organizational structures, if not whole ecosystems.

The convergent definitions presented above are convincing, but imperfect unless we say that corruption refers equally to intellectual submission, even when no financial aspect is present. In this form, it could be described as "using influence to colonize the mind." Blaise Pascal wrote: "How difficult it is to submit anything to the judgement of another, without prejudicing his judgement by the manner in which we submit it." In the same vein but more prosaically, corruption could be considered to include any action that extends a person's or entity's economic, legal, financial, or commercial influence over a state or over foreign companies by means of economic violence, fear, or ostensibly moral obligations. . . and the identity of the corrupt might not be the same as before. There is no doubt that the United States would be accused of corruption using such a definition.

NGOs, Disarming Military Arms

"Nowadays, war has disappeared as a feature of relations between developed countries. The classic elements of power are less important than the capacity to act as part of a network, to be at the center of systems of exchange and information, to master sophisticated technologies, and especially to shape the world according to an ideology and methodology that guarantee the wellbeing of a nation's population and the security of its territory. 'Coercive power relations' are less important than 'indirect structural power.'"[19]

To extend this analysis, it is worth looking in more detail at the role of groups that work to cleanse the business world and to denounce commercial activity that violates moral and ethical norms. There can be no nobler, more sacred goal. But are all the actors in this field as angelic or philanthropic as they claim? The work of the Fondation Prometheus has raised interesting questions about Transparency International,[20] which is largely funded by the Open Society, itself a project of the

[19] Jean-Michel Boucheron and Jacques Myard, *Rapport d'information parlementaire sur les vecteurs privés d'influence dans les relations internationales* (Assemblée Nationale, 2011), 29.

[20] "Dossier: ONG petit guide méthodologique à destination des journalistes… et des citoyens curieux," Lettre Prometheus (April 2016), http://www.fondation-prometheus.org/wsite/publications/newsletter/avril-2016/dossier-ong-petit-guide-m%C3%A9thodologique-%C3%A0-destination-des-journalistes/ (accessed April 18, 2017).

ultraliberal billionaire George Soros, who claims to have declared war on Old Europe.

Although there is no legal definition of what an NGO is, according to the UN Economic and Social Council[21] an NGO should not be established by a public entity or an intergovernmental agreement, and its financial resources should be mainly derived from its members' contributions. It goes without saying that it should have a nonprofit-making aim of international utility.[22] For François-Bernard Huyghe, "[NGOs'] capacity to challenge political or economic agents, but also to impose norms and to shape the agenda of public debate, gives them unprecedented power. They also have other political and economic strategies with which they seek to influence governmental decisions and to guide public opinion in ways that serve their material or ideological interests. Lobbies, think tanks, and pressure groups all also play an increasingly important role."[23]

For that reason, it is crucial to be able to separate the wheat from the chaff when it comes to these organizations—to be able to distinguish between which are acting sincerely and which serve other masters. French lawmakers have previously conducted a parliamentary inquiry into their actions.[24] One of the directors of the inquiry was Jean-Michel Boucheron, who also runs the Fondation Prometheus. It publishes an annual survey of how transparent NGOs are, judging them, gratifyingly, by the same criteria they themselves brandish at their targets. One thing that stands out from that 2011 parliamentary study is that while early NGOs (those registered with the League of Nations after 1920) did hold genuine moral principles—and often religious ones, like the Red Cross or the CCFD (Catholic Committee Against Hunger and For Development)—since the 1990s, increasing power has been wielded in the name of human rights, the environment, or the criminalization of business, by institutions with political or ideological goals. Even as far back as the 1970s, NGOs like Médecins du Monde claimed to have a "right to intervene" and preached a form of "borderlessness."[25]

The active role the NGOs have assumed is due in large part to the fact that the economy has become globalized, and that consequently states and borders have become weaker. NGOs have taken partial control of this now vacant space, clad in good intentions but profiting from the "phenomenon of the progressive secularization of charitable acts."[26] Some of the sincere ones even unwittingly play the role of "useful idiots," as in the Cold War. Their influence is considerable thanks in part to the advisory role given to them by international institutions, but also thanks to their major success stories, which with the help of a sympathetic media often achieve widespread fame.

---

[21] ECOSOC, resolution 1996/31 of July 25, 1996; see also article 71 of the 1945 UN Charter.

[22] Article 1, Convention 124 of the Council of Europe, April 27, 1986.

[23] François-Bernard Huyghe, "Influence, ONG, lobbies et réseaux,"(December 6, 2013), http://www.huyghe.fr/actu_477.htm (accessed April 18, 2017).

[24] Boucheron and Myard, Rapport d'information parlementaire.

[25] Philippe Ryfman, *Les ONG*, 3rd ed. (Paris: La Découverte, 2009), 13.

[26] Ibid., 7.

A detailed study of these organizations shows that 1,931 of the 6,846 registered NGOs (or 28.2%) are based in North America.[27] Hubert Vedrine, the former French Foreign Minister, declared in 2009 that, "only a blind person or a fool could fail to see that American and British NGOs are part of American or British soft power. . . and that they are often de facto hostile, under various pretexts, towards French influence, policies or language."[28] It is also worth noting that the top 20% most powerful NGOs receive 90% of funding.[29]

Among the most well-known NGOs that exert their influence in a wide range of ways are Transparency International, Greenpeace, Human Rights Watch, and Sherpa, but other, less familiar ones work even harder to affect deciders' choices. That was what happened at COP 21 in Paris in December 2015, when the famous WWF, accompanied by Corporate Europe Observatory, Women for a Common Culture, 350.org, Oxfam, and Les Amis de la Terre, among others, launched a direct attack on the nuclear industry. They also indirectly attacked EDF, ENGIE, and AREVA, which is majority-owned by the French state (apparently forgetting that 20% of global CO2 emissions come from American territory).[30]

In other regions, NGOs meticulously stigmatize the methods of a given company (certainly not an American one) in order to prevent it winning public contracts. This tactic is particularly beloved of United Against Nuclear Iran (UANI), which is directed by the former American ambassador to the UN. UANI works by exposing companies to public condemnation, or exerting pressure directly on Iranian company directors. Air France, Renault, Total, Engie, and Vinci are among the companies who have paid the price.[31] The tactics used leave no doubt about UANI's goal. The ultimatums they deliver to their targets never fail to mention the amounts they owe as part of deals involving American companies and/or conducted on American territory. . . we are far from Adam Smith's "invisible hand" and its distant descendants, and even further from an innocent hand. On the contrary, it shows all the signs of being a military arm.

TAFTA, or the Strategy of Containment

As for other forms of threat, the United States has seized opportunities to end bilateral treaties, in which economic agreements substitute for defense pacts, in an attempt to bypass the WTO's stalemate.[32] Just as in Asia, where the September 2015 Trans Pacific Partnership (TPP) was intended as the economic version of the military

---

[27] "Dossier: ONG petit guide méthodologique."

[28] Boucheron and Myard, *Rapport d'information parlementaire*, 20.

[29] Ryfman, *Les ONG*, 55.

[30] "COP 21: derrière l'écologie, la pression des ONG anglo-saxonnes," interview with Bernard Carayon in *Le Figaro*, September 10, 2015.

[31] Vincent Lamigeon, "L'étrange ONG américaine qui fait la chasse aux groupes français en Iran," Challenges. (August 29, 2016), https://www.challenges.fr/monde/l-etrange-ong-americaine-qui-fait-la-chasse-aux-groupes-francais-en-iran_416530 (accessed April 18, 2017).

[32] See F. Munier, "Les traités bilatéraux américans, l'autre voie de la puissance," Conflits 7 (October–November–December 2015).

ASEAN, TAFTA (Transatlantic Free Trade Agreement, also known as TTIP—Transatlantic Trade and Investment Partnership), was to be the economic counterpart of NATO, enabling its members to further increase the predominance of one economic system.[33] The economist and essayist Hervé Juvin talked of "a colonization of law" in this context.[34] It is a new American policy of containment, no longer political or military but economic. Having locked down Asia, with the notable exceptions of China and India, the United States is attempting to consolidate its economic and financial clout by imposing its own legal and commercial standards, pulling business relationships westwards so as to detach Europe more completely from what is taking place in the East. The strategy is completed by the rollback currently being inflicted on Russia. Frédéric Farah, Professor of Economics at Paris III, believes the future treaty will "definitively dilute the EU in a vast zone of free-trade, making any European political project even more difficult. I call it the ruse of history. (. . .) It is important to understand that TAFTA is intended to counteract China's rise in power."[35]

If France proved rather lackluster in negotiations, despite its volte-face in August 2016, in Germany anti-TTIP movements had already been an active force for some time. They are expertly decoded on the website infoguerre.fr, which contains reflections on the economic war.[36] The protesters' reasons for opposition included the fear that food hygiene and environmental requirements would be reduced to fall in line with the lowest existing standards, a highly sensitive subject for German environmentalists. They also denounced the way in which the negotiations were conducted. The European Commission had to be pressured before it would reveal the contents of the mandate that led to talks being established. French politicians' access to the documents was subject to draconian conditions, increasing the sense of opacity.

That this sort of international commercial act, if it ever saw the light of day, would have represented another erasure of Romano-Germanic law to the benefit of Anglo-Saxon common law is only too clear when we consider the dispute resolution mechanism that would have formed part of the treaty, known as ISDS (investor-state dispute settlement). ISDS is a disposition that would have given companies the option of taking a case to an arbitration court (that would sit in Washington and be conducted according to the American procedure and in English) to claim compensation for damages caused by national laws deemed contrary to the principles of the free trade treaty. In other words, and this cannot fail to alarm anyone who sincerely objects to the treaty, a commercial company can sue a state to claim compensation for laws that work against its economic interests, or even get those laws annulled, as has happened in the past. Other concerns include the effects on environmental and social laws or on the precautionary principle, even if such effects were constitutional. Judges would no

---

[33] "Dossier: le Traité transatlantique, un piège?" *Lettre Prometheus* (July 2015).

[34] Hervé Juvin, *Le mur de l'Ouest n'est pas tombé* (Paris: Pierre Guillaume de Roux, 2015).

[35] Interview in *Libération*, April 25, 2016.

[36] "Pourquoi la campagne anti-TTIP est-elle plus efficace en Allemagne qu'en France?" Last modified October 28, 2015, http://www.infoguerre.fr/culture-et-influence/pourquoi-la-campagne-anti-ttip-est-elle-plus-efficace-en-allemagne-quen-france-5748 (accessed April 18, 2017).

longer make judgments based on the public good, which is the principal criterion in European law, but based on commercial benefits that had allegedly been restricted by sovereign legislation.

"It is clear that economic, but also social and intellectual globalization is shaping law, and not just international law but also domestic laws."[37] The adoption of the Anglo-Saxon legal system by the European continent represents "the deployment of law as a weapon in the war of influence currently being fought by different regions, all trying to assert their own claim as the pivotal location or benchmark for business transactions."[38] During the sessions at Brussels, at which the author was a participant, it was revealed that one important element had been omitted from TAFTA: services. TAFTA's goal is the free circulation of goods, but services were quickly excluded from the negotiations because of apparently insurmountable obstacles to do with the principle of public service, a European concept that is foreign to American liberal principles. However, the Americans would not back down, and services were placed at the heart of another treaty already under discussion: the Trade in Services Agreement (TiSA). Negotiations for TiSA are as opaque as those for TAFTA, but recent revelations show that its participants are working to further liberalize all services, including non-competitive services, by imposing a blanket rule of "non-discriminatory treatment."

Taxation Cannot Escape the Economic War: Tax Havens, Foreign Account Tax Compliance Act, and Dutch Sandwiches

The revelations of the Panama Papers media scandal, when documents containing the names of private individuals who had hidden their financial assets using offshore loopholes were leaked, were bound to unleash criticism of opportunities and methods for avoiding tax. After all, is tax avoidance not simply the other side of the globalization coin and its associated practice of dumping, whether social or fiscal? Following on from this thought, it would be useful to look at tax havens in a more geopolitical light. Wherever ethics takes priority, the reality of the facts teaches us once again that we must read events within an appropriate analytical framework.

The Global Europe Anticipation Bulletin (GEAB) remarks that the United States tends to turn a blind eye to the emergence of these sorts of free tax zones, especially as certain federated states, such as Puerto Rico, are currently facing serious budgetary debt, the only way to repay which is to resort to fiscal dumping.[39] The lack of American names in the Panama Papers also makes it clear that U.S. taxpayers prefer to use tax havens within their own federal territory rather than looking further afield. Delaware can be treated as symptomatic in this respect. Its situation exposes the indulgence of the federal government, which allows one of its states to function as a tax haven within federal territory while at the same time criticizing Switzerland,

---

[37] Bertrand du Marais, "Guerre du droit, Paris brûle-t-il?," *l'ENA hors les murs* 445 (2014): 16–18.
[38] Ibid.
[39] *GEAB* 105 (2016): 27.

Monaco, or Andorra.[40]

Vincent Piolet's work in this area is extremely instructive. He shows how the implementation of legislation designed to combat tax havens (which are denounced as non-cooperative states), and the suspension of banking confidentiality on the European continent, both lead in practice to the transfer of capital to the American continent, to the benefit of fiscally lenient U.S. states. Taxation has undeniably become another weapon in the economic war.[41]

More specifically, the Foreign Account Tax Compliance Act, known as FATCA, is an extraterritorial regulation along the same lines as SOX and the FCPA (see above). As the American lawyer Stanley Ruchelman says, "the global legal system is undergoing a transformation, driven by the United States. FATCA is our weapon against tax evasion. It is the weapon of choice for democracies who want to take back control of their own revenues by making cheats pay their fair share. Countries must pick a side." Under the pretext of such ostensibly virtuous arguments, more than a hundred countries and a hundred thousand financial organizations have signed the FATCA agreement since June 2014.[42] The legislation obliges foreign banks to tell Washington the identities of any American citizens who evade the IRS.[43] While the principle of fiscal sovereignty is certainly not in itself a bad thing, the consequence of this sort of imposition on the banks is nevertheless the retention of capital within American territory, or at least its repatriation by means of fiscal procedures in order to drain currency out of the country where it was originally held.

That being the case, perhaps Europe's retaliation will take a fiscal form, following the example of Al Capone, the notorious Chicago mobster who was eventually brought down by tax evasion charges. To understand the issues at stake, we must first understand that nowadays there are two different worlds: the real economy and the financial (or digital) economy. The temptation for international corporations is to exploit the imbalance between the two by comparing different fiscal policies and choosing the most profitable. So while a product may be bought and ordered through a website in France, the shipper will be based in a more fiscally welcoming territory (like Ireland). This mechanism is even more beneficial for services (Facebook and Google) that have low material logistics requirements. Actors in the digital sector, particularly the GAFA companies,[44] take advantage of this asymmetrical situation to get around the principle of fiscal territoriality.[45] The favored process consists of a combination of two techniques, the Dutch Sandwich and the Double Irish. It works by transferring all royalty payments through a Dutch company that acts as an intermediary

---

[40] Alexandre Moustafa, "Les États-Unis, ce nouveau paradis fiscal," *Portail de l'IE*. (April 6, 2016), http://portail-ie.fr/article/1397/Les-Etats-Unis-ce-nouveau-paradis-fiscal (accessed April 18, 2017).

[41] Vincent Piolet, "Le paradis fiscal, une construction géopolitique," *Conflits* 7 (October–November–December 2015): 19–21.

[42] In France, Act 214-1098 of September 29, 2015.

[43] The US tax authority.

[44] GAFA stands for Google, Amazon, Facebook, Apple.

[45] Article 218 A of the French "Code general des impôts."

between a company based in Ireland and its parent company based in a tax haven. The accumulation of advantages available under Irish and Dutch law means that all the profits of the multinational company, which is based in Europe, can be transferred to the tax haven, where the corporate tax rate is very attractive.

On April 28, 2014, the G5 nations (France, the United Kingdom, Germany, Spain, and Italy) met to decide the fiscal fate of the Internet giants, particularly Google. Their decision was implemented in the form of increased tax audits targeting companies that are perhaps slightly too efficient at exploiting disparities in national legislation between the member states. Google was subjected to a significant tax audit in France, the result of which was that it was ordered to pay a billion euros in extra tax. Amazon, Facebook, and Apple are undergoing similar procedures.[46] The OECD, for its part, has initiated discussions about how to tax the digital economy as part of its BEPS (base erosion and profit shifting) plan.

Since 2014, Margrethe Vestager, European Commissioner for Competition, has made it her personal mission to utilize the sanction procedure provided for cases where a company abuses a dominant position. A notable instance was the case against Google's Android system.[47] This almost unforeseen turn of events forced Amazon to alter its structural fiscal policy, which it centralized in Luxembourg. In future, the distributor will account for the profits it makes in each member state separately. Finally, there was a serious showdown between the European Union and Facebook regarding the use of personal data.

Cyberspace, A New Sphere of Confrontation and Sovereignty

In this area too, the response came from the European judges. The Court of Justice of the European Union (CJEU),[48] enjoying what amounted to an unexpected retrieval of power, delivered a judgment that represented a slap in the face to the American authorities. After the revelations of "digital spying" that came to light during the Snowden scandal, an Austrian Internet user became worried that American antiterrorism laws[49] could authorize the NSA or the FBI to examine personal data collected through his Facebook account. Although Facebook's European headquarters are actually in Ireland for the tax reasons discussed above, the data it collects are exported, saved, and processed through data centers based in the United States, and are thus under the jurisdiction of the American authorities and subject to its intelligence agencies.

The Austrian man appealed to the Irish courts (although not before his first application was rejected by the Data Protection Commissioner) and the Irish High Court referred the question to the CJEU. The trial was suspended until the supreme

[46] The European Union is reclaiming thirteen billion euros in back taxes from Apple.

[47] Sylvain Rolland, "Comment l'Europe veut mettre les GAFA au pas," *Libération* (May 28, 2015).

[48] Aff. C-362/14 of October 6, 2015.

[49] The Patriot Act, later the Freedom Act.

jurisdiction had interpreted the rule. The CJEU's task was, based on the analysis of relevant personal data protection standards, to come to a decision about Directive 95/46. Under the terms of this directive, particularly Article 28, every EU member state must establish an authority for protecting personal data, and citizens must have access to appeal procedures with regard to the use and exploitation of their data. It also provides for arrangements to guarantee a certain level of security for the personal data of EU citizens. Because data from Facebook accounts are centrally stored in American territory, the CJEU reexamined Decision 2000/520/EC of July 26, 2000, which deemed the American "Safe Harbor" framework to be adequate to satisfy the requirements of Directive 95/46. The question facing the CJEU was whether Safe Harbor could actually guarantee the implementation of data protection rules that were compatible with European standards. In its judgment of October 6, 2015, the CJEU decided that the United States did not offer sufficient guarantee for the security of the personal data of EU citizens. Consequently, Safe Harbor was declared ineffective under the terms of European confidentiality rules as set out in Directive 95/46. Soon afterwards, fierce negotiations began about a new agreement called "EU-US Privacy Shield." News of the negotiations went public on February 4, 2016. There are still numerous exceptions, particularly in terms of stricter requirements for cooperating with international corruption (FCPA) and personal tax (FATCA) investigations.

In the same spirit, France's National Committee for Information and Liberty (CNIL) and four other European authorities published a joint declaration—that was also an injunction—on the subject of Facebook's intensive use of cookies. It referred to security rules imposed on users of the website with regard to the publication of personal information. In particular, Facebook was criticized by Belgium for having tracked users even outside its own website. Likewise, the "data protection package" of July 8, 2016, designed to provide an efficient framework that would guarantee a high level of data protection within the EU, had to ensure that EU citizens were able to control their personal information in a way that prevented it being misused by "international companies operating on the internet."

It was not a comprehensive or definitive response, and it dealt with the question of the protection of EU citizens' personal data with caution. Nevertheless, it raised real awareness about the way in which private information is used. It was recently backed up by the Court of Appeal in Paris, which declared itself competent to judge in the matter of the publication of a photograph on a Facebook account, dismissing the fact that the social network's terms and conditions of use specify American jurisdiction.[50] So, it is indeed in the digital sphere that Europe has decided to launch its counterattack.

This begging of the question will suffice if we remember the words of former U.S. President Barack Obama in February 2015, spoken in response to accusations of digital espionage. He announced boldly that the United States had created and shared the Internet, and that it therefore owned the information that the Internet merely

[50] TGI Paris, ruling of March 5, 2015, confirmed by the Court of Appeal in Paris on February 12, 2016.

borrowed. The ongoing reform of ICANN[51] reveals the United States' reluctance to relinquish their hold.[52]

And yet, there are still overt actions and goals of liberation to be found. For example:

- Actions taken and sanctions envisaged by the European Union against Manuel Barroso, former President of the European Commission, following his recruitment by the commercial bank Goldman Sachs.[53]
- Tightening of visa requirements between Europe and the United States.
- Adoption by Germany and France of anti-TAFTA positions in September 2016 (which did not, however, represent a fundamental challenge to the mandate given to the European Union).
- Revisiting the idea of a European defense system outside NATO, discussed at the European Summit in Bratislava in September 2016.[54]

The struggle for independence seems to be well and truly underway—unless the result of the recent U.S. presidential election manages to consign the arrogant, defeated neoconservatives to the background on its own.

[51] The organization that manages Internet domain names, itself under the control of the American government.

[52] Benjamin Ferran, "La France critique la mainmise durable des Etats-Unis sur Internet," Le Figaro (March 24, 2016).

[53] Goldman Sachs had manipulated Greece's accounts in order for it to be able to adopt the Euro, which was then itself weakened by Greece.

[54] Following Turkey's decision to leave NATO.

Special Report -"Imperialism's New Clothes" Exploring the Idea of Influence in Economic Warfare: From Fair Competition to Criminal Conspiracies

Bruno Racouchot[A]

When leaders determine their political and economic strategies, they always take key parameters like influence, seduction, guile, manipulation, and deliberate disinformation into account—that is, they rely on all the usual tools of soft power, which combine with those of hard power to form an extremely effective offensive line. This has been the approach since time immemorial, even if the concepts it presses into service have, of course, evolved over time.

As researcher and journalist Ali Laïdi explains:

> "From Stone Age conflicts to the NSA's mass economic surveillance, very little has really changed. What we have is an evolution of form, as the weapons being used in these constant economic struggles evolve. Human beings have always sought to protect their own means of subsistence, and to annex those of others. During the Neolithic period, exchanges did not exist as such; violence was the only means available to seize the surplus amassed by other groups or to drive them away from fertile territory. In antiquity, people relied on cunning, secrets, and lies to settle their trade disputes. The Middle Ages saw the rise of the merchant. Bypassing state structures altogether, merchants banded together in a network of cities, forming powerful trade leagues capable of imposing their privileges, organiszing economic blockades, and even declaring war on anyone threatening their interests."[1]

Globalization has led to an unprecedented proliferation of all these traditional methods. There are no spaces remote enough, no time frames too small for these

---

[A] Bruno Racouchot holds a DEA in Defense and International Relations from the Sorbonne and is the director of *Comes Communication* (www.comes-communication.com), a communications company based in Paris, Toronto (Canada), São Paulo and Porto Alegre (Brazil). It specializes in an influence-centered type of communication based on the promotion of strong identities. The company works in close collaboration with experts in strategic planning, management and branding. Bruno Racouchot is also the editor of *Communication & Influence*, a monthly newsletter, and of the blog www.communicationetinfluence.fr

[1] Ali Laïdi, *Histoire mondiale de la guerre économique* (Paris: Perrin, 2016), cited in "Puissance et influence dans la guerre économique : le décryptage d'Ali Laïdi", *Communication & Influence* 76 (September 2016): 3.

polymorphic strategies, that work to destabilize political and economic power relations, affecting them in positive or negative ways. Most people tend to equate these methods to a form of manipulation, of disinformation, even of propaganda, words which bring to mind the Cold War era! English and American writers, who use the word "influence" to mean a set of techniques compelling its objects to make decisions that are not in their own best interest, have only served to reinforce this negative perception.

Influence can also, however, be viewed in a more positive light, as a means to open up new horizons. As Alain Juillet points out: "influence makes it possible to convince people to consider new points of view, to change their own thought paradigms, to revise their basic principles." He then adds:

> "What brings about this shift is the new evidence they find themselves confronted with, and that forces them to rethink. In short, one could say that the more intelligent a person is, the easier he/she will be to influence, precisely because influence presupposes a certain analytical ability, and requires people to differentiate between what they "usually" think and the new material presented to them, which they must analyze to see if it is valid. Any sound argument can therefore lead them to revise their conclusions, and, thereby, to alter their own position. That is where the process of influence begins."[2]

As François-Bernard Huyghe puts it, "influence, which always works conjointly with other forms of power, triggers a series of shifts and replacements. It compels people to change their words or actions, without relying on force, quid pro quos, contracts, or any other form of coercion. It shifts the center of gravity of power."[3]

Let us then consider how these strategies of influence, both positive or negative, express themselves concretely in the sphere of economic warfare, and how they end up disrupting established practices, altering power relations, and generating significant returns on investment for those relying on them.

The Vital Role of Influence in Economic Competition

To find an example of how influence can be used in a positive way, we need look no further than Harley Davidson's excellent high-end branding, exemplified by the music video *Live by it*.[4] Although Harley Davidson sells motorcycles, what they really are in the business of selling is the American dream. In this video, there is

---

[2] Alain Juillet, *Communication & Influence*, Hors-Série 1 (June 2009): 1-2.
[3] François-Bernard Huyghe, *Maîtres du faire croire* (Paris: Vuibert, 2008), 9.
[4] See http://www.dailymotion.com/video/x9hho3_great-harley-davidson-film-harley-d_auto

no mention of the motorcycles' technical advantages, the focus is rather on certain core values that speak of the American west in the popular imagination. They are expressed through a series of words and images that show a group of bikers' epic ride through various mythical American landscapes, and that conveys a strong sense of a community bound together by common values. Harley Davidson deliberately draws on the mythical aura of its products and on the cultural associations triggered by the company name. What a video like this one goes to show is that in the realm of economic warfare, victory does not belong to the companies that have the best products (the video makes no claims about the company's superior quality or technology) or to those whose products deliver the best performances, but rather to those companies who benefit from the positive public image forged by their own powerful identities.

Emerging countries reached this conclusion a long time ago, which is why they have often relied on their best-performing domestic companies as a spearhead to conquer Western markets. Brazil is an interesting case in this regard. Very early on, General Golbery do Couto e Silva let this idea shape his overall geopolitical policy and his plans for the country's future, in close collaboration with the Itamaraty, Brazil's Ministry of External Relations.

However, far from remaining the prerogative of Brazil's military and diplomatic personnel, the tools of soft power are now also wielded by the companies that have joined in the government's efforts. In the words of geographer Hervé Théry, who knows the country in and out, "these companies, that have recently stepped onto the international scene, play an increasingly active and influential part; having shed their initial passivity, they now seem to be unhampered by any third-world inferiority complex. Many entrepreneurs from the agribusiness, mining, and manufacturing sectors actively seek to conquer foreign markets." By skillfully exploiting all the images traditionally associated with Brazil in the popular consciousness (beaches, pretty girls, music, football, a certain zest for life, and a generally dynamic outlook), private actors have greatly contributed to strengthening Brazil's foreign influence; these include "major multinational corporations like Embraer, la Vale, or Petrobras, but also large medium-sized companies that know how to use the country's selling points and that have acquired significant shares of the market in certain niche sectors."[5]

In addition to appealing to the popular imagination, there are also other ways of exerting influence, for instance by relying on rational arguments, or by seeking to spread certain types of knowledge, in order to gain a competitive advantage, or to shift the balance of power in the economic field. Based on the descriptions of Pierre Fayard, a specialist of Sun-Tsu, this appears to be the case in certain Japanese knowledge communities. Fayard points out that "in Japan, information is action, which is why the relational space that links together facts, objects, and living things is the focus of attention, for this malleable vacuity is the matrix of everything that will be, or rather, of everything that is in the process of becoming."[6]

---

[5] Hervé Théry, *Le Brésil, pays émergé* (Armand Colin, 2014), 188-190.

[6] Pierre Fayard, Le réveil du samouraï: culture et stratégie japonaises dans la société de la connaissance (Dunod, 2007),153

Pierre Fayard further argues:

> "In the evolution of these strategic knowledge communities, [we can see] a clear break with the usual way in which an organization relates to its field. Structurally hybrid, these organizations adapt to a constantly changing reality by collaborating to find the best solutions. Twenty-first century clients and users are educated and well-informed, they communicate with each other, exchange views and information and thereby also broaden each other's horizons. To forget this is to forgo the chance of drawing on their collective intelligence. Because the interaction between them is so rich, it triggers a wealth of creativity, which does not benefit a single actor, but rather the entire company with its community of clients and users. In a world where value increasingly springs from the ability to produce knowledge, the "together" strategy appears to win over the "against" strategy."[7]

Working "together," however, is only possible where there is a common intellectual ground, which, in turn, presupposes an ability to debate, to think together, and to legitimately seek to influence others in order to win them over.

Let us turn to a French example of how influence can be exerted through the diffusion of knowledge, and in this specific case through the Grenoble School of Management's 2009 decision to organize a Geopolitical Festival, and to set up a website on which students and staff—but also external actors like managers or business executives looking for synthetic information on areas of strategic interest to them—can access a series of geopolitical analysis notes, known as CLES, *Comprendre les Enjeux Stratégiques* (Understanding Strategic Issues).[8] By establishing a connection between the institution and the field of geopolitics, this initiative has helped to make the school more attractive to potential students.

In one of the aforementioned CLES papers, the geographer and former ambassador Michel Foucher highlights the interconnection between geopolitics, geoeconomics, and influence strategies. He argues that:

> "Influence is really a form of geopolitics and cannot be reduced to the simple idea of promoting French culture abroad. People turn to France because they are looking for a different way of discussing world issues, one that does not conform to the standard discourse of Western globalization. That is why it is so important to visibly participate in international intellectual debates. Many countries expect France to defend a rather different, more Tocquevillian

[7] Fayard, *Le réveil du samouraï*, 223.
[8] Accessible at http://notes-geopolitiques.com/

> position in their foreign policy. They are routinely disappointed, however, because this expectation is not in line with France's current, very American-centered positioning on a number of issues."[9]

Ideas and intellectual debate play a key role in the implementation of influence strategies, an idea that I will return to presently. So, for instance, it is hardly a coincidence if Michel Foucher has also edited an *Atlas de l'influence française* (*Atlas of French Influence*), which includes contributions from more than 50 specialists who outline the various facets of France's international influence. In the introduction, significantly entitled "Power and Influence, Benchmark and Standard" (Puissance et influence, repère et référence), Michel Foucher argues that today, power strategies need to work hand in hand with influence strategies, and that no entirely political approach can be successful if it does not also seek to integrate economic initiatives:

> "What we learn from the French experience is that public policies of influence are typically developed and adopted at critical historical junctures, in order to compensate for what can no longer be obtained through traditional power strategies, and to restore the country's position in a changing world. It would be misguided to believe that a state's image only depends on its economic performance. Attempts to reduce foreign policy to a mere promotional campaign designed to sell "the French brand" overlook everything that France has brought to the world and everything that it still has to contribute."[10]

Influence as a Key Weapon in Information Warfare

An important thing to bear in mind when considering notions like soft, smart, or soft power, is that in the end, they can all be boiled down to two things: might and power. Claude Revel, a former interministerial delegate in charge of economic intelligence, has repeatedly insisted on the fact that influence must be understood as a weapon, that is, as a means of acquiring power over other people, and of annihilating differing opinions in order to replace them with the bearer's own views.[11] In its "light" version, influence can be understood as the ability to control other actors—and even entire systems—in order to defend one's own interests and to achieve certain ends.

In the 1990s, Joseph Nye introduced the notion of soft power, the idea that

[9] Michel Foucher, interviewed by Michel Fiorina, "Géopolitique de l'influence: Michel Fiorina s'entretient avec Michel Foucher", CLES: *Comprendre les Enjeux Stratégiques* 32 (February 2014): 3. http://notes-geopolitiques.com/wp-content/uploads/2014/02/CLESHS32.pdf

[10] Foucher and Fiorina, "Géopolitique de l'influence", 13.

[11] Claude Revel, *La France, un pays sous influence?* (Paris: Vuibert, 2012).

a nation's influence cannot be reduced to the power wielded by the state, but also stems from its ability to fascinate and attract outsiders by its culture, its values, or its way of life. Claude Revel has devoted a lot of attention to the exorbitant power wielded by norms that force us to submit, like the Romans at the battle of the Caudine Forks, to the conditions and criteria laid out by their creators, often with their own personal interests in mind. Business lawyer, Olivier de Maison Rouge, adopts a similar approach in a recent article entitled "The Geopolitics of Law: The Other Battlefield of Economic Warfare" (*La géopolitique du droit: l'autre champ de bataille de la guerre économique*).[12]

Projecting an attractive image, appealing to the imagination, invoking reason, spreading knowledge, establishing norms, and applying regulations are all important components of soft power strategies, which are immensely influential since they determine how tomorrow's battles will be fought. They amount to a form of mental conditioning. Hence the central importance of information warfare.

A 2006 report from the General Secretariat for National Defense highlights what is at stake in this information war:

> "There are many allusions in the economic game to technical or financial information being manipulated for specific ends. What the word "manipulation" brings to mind are various schemes designed to deliberately misrepresent reality by altering certains aspects of it, and to exploit these changes in order to gain influence. Such destabilizing strategies are designed to alter an earlier equilibrium and to impact the activity of the persons, groups, or organizations at which they are targeted negatively."[13]

What complicates matters is the sheer scale of today's information society. A range of new actors have emerged alongside traditional forces:

> "Civil society is increasingly getting involved in the economic and political game. Typically opting for the underdog approach, civil society groups rely to a great extent on highly targeted, Internet-based actions, particularly suited to small groups with little manpower and few technical means at their disposal. This has allowed non-governmental organizations, unions and associations benefiting from a positive public image and enjoying an increasing degree of legitimacy to make their voice heard

[12] Olivier de Maison Rouge, "La géopolitique du droit: l'autre champ de bataille de la guerre économique", *Syndicat Français de l'Intelligence Economique* (newsletter) 5 (March 2016): 10-3 http://synfie.fr/index.php/actualites/lettre-trimestrielle/finish/5-lettre/500-lettre-d-information-du-synfie-mars-2016 p.10

[13] Secrétariat général de la Défense nationale, *Synthèse générale du groupe de travail sur les manipulations de l'information stratégique dans le domaine économique et financier* (October 2006), 1.

> on the world stage in order to further their ends. Manipulating information is one of the strategies relied on by pragmatic and voluntarist public actors, who seek to increase their own influence by launching information campaigns designed to protect their own economic and industrial interests."[14]

Harming Some People, Deceiving the Rest: The Dark Side of Influence

All this has led to the rise of a new tool in the scramble for power: influence communication. As we have seen, it can be used for positive ends, as when an organization seeks to promote its own distinctive identity or brand in order to attract customers, partners, or new adherents. It can also be put to more nefarious ends, however, like seeking to influence institutions or to weigh in on various processes, especially of a legislative or regulatory nature. In its darkest guise, influence communication can, as Eric Delbecque and Christian Harbulot point out, have devastating effects:

> "Slowly but surely [it can] undermine the image or reputation of the targeted actor. Anti-smoking campaigns, for instance, provide us with a prime example of this, since they have managed to tarnish the image of the tobacco industry permanently. The various strategies that form the heart of influence communication are both very hard to define and difficult to counteract, since they are not technically illegal. Yet this specific subset of the strategies of influence communication warrants our full attention, because this is what we mean by "information warfare.". These days, anticipating this type of attacks is compulsory for any organization wishing to control its image and to safeguard its reputation."[15]

Criminal organizations, for one, have long ago understood the potential of soft power to extend and increase their operations. Just in the last few years, we have witnessed every conceivable variation on the use of influence communication for criminal ends. Police superintendent Jean-François Gayraud provides a detailed analysis of these strategies in his recent work *L'art de la guerre financière* (*The Art of Financial Warfare*).[16] He shows, for instance, how remarkably efficient it can be to rely on a "providential fog" of communication and information in order to throw sand into the eyes of one's opponents or of the authorities. What this strategy does is to distort images, rather than to blur vision itself.

Dissecting the laws of financial counterfeiting, Jean-François Gayraud

---

[14] Synthèse générale, 1-2.
[15] Eric Delbecque and Christian Harbulot, *La guerre économique* (Paris: PUF, 2010), 59.
[16] Jean-François Gayraud, *L'art de la guerre financière* (Odile Jacob, 2016).

particularly highlights the importance of the first of them, the ability to make false statements in order to carry out real acts of predation.[17] The aim, as he explains, is to forge false theories and concepts that can then be used to underpin future criminal operations, and to endow them with an aura of legitimacy.

Following this logic, financial predators have invented a form of "newspeak" designed to conceal their operations. As Jean-François Gayraud points out, the best way of altering reality is to give a carefully slanted description of it. The aim is nothing short of restricting the very boundaries of thought. Hence, their reliance on a pretentious jargon that conceals cynical operations of large-scale predation under a gloss of professional and academic respectability.[18]

Criminal organizations are fully aware of the subtle links that exist between influence and power, and know that combining them can yield astounding results. The rise of this arsenal of soft power has radically altered existing power relations, as Eric Delbecque convincingly explains:

> "In the past, a nation's firepower determined its international standing. Influence strategies could complement a nation's military moves on the international chessboard, but they were only of secondary importance. Today, the opposite is true: influence strategies do not only reflect, but also shape the very nature of the confrontations between different actors in the many spheres where human collectivities, cultural models, and private organizations compete. The aim is no longer to aggressively overcome rivals, but rather to gently rob them of their freedom of movement (in a stealthy and perfectly hypocritical way), to restrict their choices, to limit their possibilities and their earning prospects by subtly altering the global environment in which they evolve, in order to bring about their gradual downfall, all the while cementing one's own supremacy."[19]

Concluding Remarks

All this points to the central importance of three key parameters, which represent as many conundrums:

> 1. People underestimate the essential role played by ideas in the power games set in motion by political and economic challenges.

---

[17] Gayraud, *L'art de la guerre financière*, 91.

[18] Gayraud, *L'art de la guerre financière*, 116-117.

[19] Eric Delbecque, L'influence ou les guerres secrètes, (Paris: Vuibert, 2011), 17 ; for another work on the same issue see Christian Harbulot, *La main invisible des puissances* (Paris: Ellipses, 2007).

> 2. In a similar way, they do not realize the important role played by communication strategies in these power games.
>
> 3. Keeping these blind spots in mind is essential if we wish to become more aware of our weaknesses. If we forget the importance of influence strategies, we cannot formulate and implement our own strategies.

1. As Jean-François Gayraud points out, what makes predation possible in the first place is the ideas that give it a veneer of legitimacy and thereby help to conceal it. Everything begins with ideas, and here Gayraud cites John Maynard Keynes' General Theory in support of his claims: "The ideas of economists and political philosophers, both when they are right and when they are wrong, are more powerful than is commonly understood. Indeed the world is ruled by little else. Practical men, who believe themselves to be quite exempt from any intellectual influence, are usually the slaves of some defunct economist."[20] To grasp the logic of criminal actions, it is essential to first understand the intentions behind them, and to that end, to recognize the central importance of thought. Hence, the pressing need to rid ourselves of our "technological fetishism," which is all the more problematic as our comfortable and naive trust in technology's ability to find answers keeps us from venturing into the perilous realm of thought. In this sense influence can, as we saw earlier with Alain Juillet, be viewed in a positive light as an attempt to revive classical rhetoric, and to defend freedom of thought against intellectual conformity.[21]

2. The second aporia pertains to the tendency, among specialists of economic intelligence, to routinely overlook the importance of communication. This shortcoming has already been pointed out by Thierry Libaert and Nicolas Moinet, who have shown that communication and information-sharing systems are of pivotal importance for today's organizations.[22] Either out of complacency or fear, however, most actors in the field of economic intelligence appear reluctant to take this parameter into account, a tendency that Alain Juillet and I have already criticized:

> "In France, the world of communication and that of economic intelligence hardly overlap. They are shockingly ignorant about each other, relying as they do on a crude set of preconceptions made up of stereotypes and even of caricatures. Communication specialists tend to view economic intelligence as a suspicious activity for spooks, taking place in smoke-filled backrooms,

[20] John Maynard Keynes, *The General Theory of Employment, Interest and Money* (London: Macmillan, 1976), 383.

[21] Alain Juillet and Bruno Racouchot, "Les stratégies d'influence ou la liberté de l'esprit face à la pensée convenue", *Revue Internationale d'Intelligence Economique* 4 (2012):.89-102.

[22] Thierry Libaert and Nicolas Moinet, "La communication, dimension oubliée de l'intelligence économique", Communication & Organisation 42 (2012): 161-74.

> whilst economic intelligence actors contemptuously dismiss communication work as glitzy and superficial. The persistence of this type of divide based on fiction rather than fact is all the more surprising as we live in a time when the creation, circulation, integration, and processing of information represent a key component of success in the fields of politics, economics, and culture alike. As such, it also prevents us from successfully defending and promoting our interests."[23]

3. The last and most important of these three aporias is the strategic void that afflicts us, and that has been described in such striking terms by Philippe Baumard.[24] To face the challenges of the modern world and those that still lie in store for us, we need to open our eyes and to once again learn how to think critically. Strategy is nothing less than "the ability to define a fundamental purpose—an intent—that safeguards not only what is, but also what will be, while setting out the conditions for their successful growth."[25] The new game of ideas that influence has set in motion requires us to seriously engage with fundamental ontological issues. We cannot claim that we wish to be part of this world if we do not also seek to truly understand who we are and what it is we want to achieve. Like all great periods of transformation, the crisis that looms ahead of us, wreathed in the smoke of war, could also prove to be a chance of rebirth. In the words of Hölderlin, where there is danger, there grows also that which saves.

---

[23] Alain Juillet et Bruno Racouchot, "L'influence, le noble art de l'intelligence économique", in "La communication, dimension oubliée de l'intelligence économique", *Communication & Organisations*, n° 42, Presses universitaires de Bordeaux, 2012, p. 161

[24] Philippe Baumard, *Le vide stratégique* (CNRS, 2012).

[25] Baumard, Le vide stratégique, p.15-16.

The Use of Homemade Bombs (Explosive or Incendiary) in France: A Dangerous Development

Patricia Lucat[A]

Homemade bombs, or IEDs (improvised explosive devices), are not a new invention. However, a look at current events shows that the use of such bombs has been growing for several years, particularly in connection with minority activist groups determined to disturb public order and threaten social stability. Against the background of a high terrorism threat, radical Islamists are the most numerous users of these explosive devices, while protests (for example, against French labor law) provide anarchists with an opportunity to demonstrate their disruptive power. Finally, homemade bombs are also a powerful and dangerous tool for criminals.

The threat is significantly increased by the sharing of formulas for explosive chemicals on the Internet and by the widespread commercial availability of precursor products. Individuals, often young, are now able to make homemade bombs—a worrying development, especially in the context of radicalization. But some countries have started to react: for example, Belgium has recently restricted the sale of precursor chemicals.

Homemade Bombs Used in Terrorism

In its digital, photographically illustrated magazine *Inspire* (June 2010), al-Qaeda explained how to "Make a bomb in the kitchen of your mom." That article helped Dzhokhar Tsarnaev, one of the two Boston bombers, make the explosive devices that killed three people at the Boston marathon on April 15, 2013.

Homemade bombs are the favored weapon of terrorists, especially those of Islamic State. TATP, the explosive compound used by the suicide bombers in the attacks in Paris (November 2015) and Brussels (March 2016), is easy to make, although it is unstable. The ingredients it contains—acetone peroxide, oxygenated water, and sulfuric acid—are widely commercially available. Even if making TATP requires some skill, buying the materials is "child's play."[1]

Eight hundred grams of red phosphorus, a highly inflammable substance that can be bought legally on the Internet, were found in August at the home of a radicalized individual in Brussels. He claimed it was for use in scientific experiments.

[A] Patricia Lucat holds a degree in Contemporary History and a Master of Public Law specializing in homeland security. She has held a teaching post since 2001, and since 2008 she has worked as a media monitor at the risk management firm Aconit, focusing on threats currently facing businesses and local communities.

[1] *Europe 1*, 12/11/15.

In July 2016, explosives were also found during a search of the home of a 23-year-old radicalized individual who worked as a driver for a French tourism company. The quantities involved are sometimes enormous. At the end of March 2016, fifteen 15 kilograms of explosives, 15 liters of acetone, 30 liters of hydrogen peroxide, and several detonators were found during a search in Brussels. Also in March, but in France this time, TATP and weapons were found in Argenteuil (Val d'Oise) at the home of a suspect whose attack plans were, according to the French interior minister, "advanced."[2]

It is not just Islamists who use homemade bombs. The authorities, especially in France, have been concerned for some years about extreme left-wing terrorism directed at the symbols or agents of the state (for example, by anarchists and autonomists). In recent years, left-wing groups have carried out attacks at sites of social conflict. These include ZADs (Zones to Defend), unofficial camps established in order to prevent large-scale projects such as the extension of the Notre Dame des Landes airport (Loire-Atlantique), as well as protests against French labor law or demonstrations in support of migrants. Activist violence on such occasions is limitless, and explosives—chiefly Molotov cocktails—have become part of their standard tactics.

The risks are consequently very high for police officers, who are often the first to be targeted. In left-wing ideology, slogans such as "un flic = une balle, un comico = une rafale" (a cop = a bullet, a police station = a hail of bullets) or ACAB (all cops are bastards) speak for themselves. In Toulouse on June 2, 2016, eight police officers were wounded by homemade bombs while confronting protesters who were demonstrating against the labor law and trying to surround the town center. As well as the explosive compound itself, those bombs also contained screws or nails that were fired out with great force when the bombs exploded.

In Paris on June 14, a protester was seriously wounded in the back by a projectile of this type thrown by activists. Patrice Ribeiro, secretary general of the police union Synergie-Officiers (VSD, June 30, 2016), described the incident: "We were confronted by groups operating at the margins of armed conflict. They ranged from militant antifa [anti-fascists] to the sort of itinerant extreme-left activists you often find at protests. During the demonstration, we observed the use of homemade bombs containing nails and bolts. We also recovered some bottles of acid."

Frédéric Lagache, secretary general of the police union Alliance, suggests that the escalation of anarchist anti-police violence is caused by activists developing "a sense of impunity, because the criminal justice response is almost nonexistent. These individuals spend a night in a police cell and receive at most a judicial summons—and rarely more than a warning. Attacking the police is turning into a game."[3] Few suspects are actually detained in prison, and frequent cases of assailants being released "under court supervision" cause outrage among the law enforcement authorities, who denounce the "disastrous message" it sends to "all who still want to attack police

[2] *France TV info*, 03/25/16.
[3] *Valeurs Actualles*, 07/15/16.

officers."[4]

On October 8, around 15 thugs launched a full-blown ambush on two police cars in Viry-Châtillon (Essonne). The police officers were guarding a surveillance camera that had been installed to prevent thefts from moving vehicles at a roundabout in front of the troubled housing estate of La Grande Borne. Local thugs had tried to sabotage the camera twice in one week, notably by ramming a vehicle into it. That evening, they broke the police car windows and threw Molotov cocktails inside the car. To stop the police officers getting out, the assailants blocked the car doors. A 28-year-old police community support officer was in a life-threatening condition for a long time. A 39-year-old peace officer and mother of three children sustained serious burn injuries.

A similar attack had previously taken place in July 2016, when three GPIS (Groupement parisien inter-bailleurs de surveillance) security agents were wounded, one of them seriously, during a patrol in the 20th arrondissement in Paris. About 10 individuals broke the window of their vehicle with a rock and then threw an incendiary device inside. When the agents exited the burning Renault Scenic, the group pursued them and threw homemade mortars at them.

Three such attacks in just a few months is a worryingly high rate. And mortar-throwing is developing into a common practice in deprived areas; in some cases, shotguns are even fired, as happened in Beaumont-sur-Oise after the death of Adama Traoré in July 2016.

Traoré's death on July 19, following his arrest for violence and threatening behavior outside a city council in Beaumont-sur-Oise (Val d'Oise), triggered five nights of armed rioting that shook the neighborhood of Boyenval. During the riots, police officers were shot at with hunting rifles about 60 times; 13 law enforcement agents were wounded. When two of Traoré's brothers were arrested on November 23, there was more violence. About 10 individuals made the passengers and driver disembark from a bus before throwing incendiary devices inside, destroying the vehicle and six other cars in the vicinity. Despite receiving several calls, the fire service was unable to intervene due to the number of stones being thrown.

The neighborhood of Courneuve (Seine-Saint-Denis) has also been in a state of unrest since the death of an American Staffordshire terrier. The guard dog was not on a lead and was killed by police officers after it bit them during an arrest for drug trafficking at the end of July. A video of the dog's death recorded by local residents stirred up tension in the Cité des 4000 housing estate and provoked "retaliatory action." A bus and about 20 municipal vehicles were burnt. A second bus was attacked in the same way on October 22.

Terror, intimidation… the attacks continue. There are documents circulating on the Internet that teach leftist militants or novice jihadists how to cause the most possible damage. There were about 15 cases of homemade explosive or incendiary devices being used in 2015, and there have been about 20 since the beginning of

[4] *Le Figaro*, 10/25/16

2016. They have been used during protests, at sporting events, during neighborhood disputes, by vandals or during robberies.

Terrorism, Violent Activism, and Criminality

Easy access to bomb-making "tutorials" on the Internet poses serious problems. On July 31, 2016, a 26-year-old man lost one hand and suffered severe injuries to the other while trying to make a bomb in Boisse, a municipality in Ain. On June 21, 2016, three explosions were heard in Ferrière-La-Grande (Nord), where some minors had used hydrochloric acid to make bombs in a bedroom after seeing a video on the Internet, and then threw the devices outside. They survived unscathed, but on February 11, 2016, a 28-year-old man was seriously injured in the leg in similar circumstances in Villers-Louis (Yonne).

In June 2015, three adolescents died in Bas-en-Basset (Haute-Loire) while handling the precursor chemicals for smoke bombs they planned to use in an open air war game. A fourth was seriously injured. An expert emphasized: "The two ingredients can be bought cheaply in shops and easily assembled, but they are very difficult to control… In large quantities, they could blow your house up."[5] Traces of acetone and hydrochloric acid were found at the location. After an incident in Paris in 2003, when a young man was severely injured, chemists emphasized the effectiveness of bomb recipes that are available on the internetInternet and that do not require any specialist material. One of them said, "you could learn how to blow a building up by just following the instructions."[6]

Makers of such bombs risk their own lives, certainly—but they also pose a danger to others, because once they have made the bomb they then try it out. The line between vandalism and threats to people is a thin one. Placed in public roads, thrown near public transport or stores, the risk is considerable:

- July 2016, about twenty 20 suspicious bottles were recovered in a public park next to a school group in Bois-Guillaume (Seine-Maritime) near Rouen. Some of them had already exploded.

- June 2016, three youths were arrested in Le Havre (Seine-Maritime) in possession of homemade bombs; in Villeneuve-Saint-Georges (Val-de-Marne), two adolescents were caught in the act of making an incendiary bomb in a bottle near the school they both attended.

- May 27, students took an explosive device into a school in

[5] *Le Journal du Dimanche*, 06/16/16.
[6] *Ina-Journal TF1*, 11/11/2003.

Bessancourt (Val d'Oise), where it exploded but did not harm anyone.

- In February, a washing machine in a laundromat in Viry-Noureuil (Aisne) was destroyed by an explosive device. Fortunately, there was nobody in the laundromat at the time.

- January 2016, an individual was apprehended in Decazeville (Aveyron) after having left an explosive device near a Carrefour Contact store; two high-school students were formally investigated after two explosions at their school in Limas (Rhône). Three minors were arrested in possession of explosive devices in Toulouse (Haute-Garonne) on New Year's Eve. A few days later, five youths were apprehended in Lannion (Côtes d'Armor) after an explosion in a public road.

- December 2015, three youths were apprehended in Mont-de-Marsan (Gers) after having caused two explosions in a street and a public park.

- November 2015, three adolescents were arrested with a homemade bomb in Laon (Aisne).

- October 2015, a hypermarket in Beaubreuil, near Limoges (Haute-Vienne), was targeted by two bombs. The second device was discovered before it exploded, but the store had to be evacuated when the first went off, although it did not cause any damage. A 9-year-old child was apprehended.

- September 2015, an explosion went off in the middle of the road in Arques (Pas-de-Calais). A dangerous bomb fired out a handful of nails. There were no passersby in the area.

- August 2015, three youths from Quetigny (Côte d'Or) were arrested for having made explosive devices and thrown them at the tramway, near pedestrians and cyclists.

- July 2015, a homemade device exploded in a public restroom in a park in Nancy.

- May 2015, five adolescents, aged from thirteen13 to fifteen15, from Vaulx-en-Velin (Rhône), were summoned to appear before a judge for having thrown homemade bombs at pedestrians and cars.

- April 2015, a high-school student was apprehended after having left two explosive bottles on a bus in Toulouse (Haute-Garonne).

- January 2015, a homemade bomb exploded in front of a kebab van near a mosque in Villefranche-sur-Saône (Rhône). As it was not long after the Charlie Hebdo attack, the police treated it as a retaliatory attack.

IEDs are also used at sporting events. There were explosions during the UEFA Euro 2016 championship, notably on June 18 at a match between Iceland and Hungary. Although security had been increased in view of the terrorist threat, an explosive device was brought into Marseille stadium on June 13 during a match between England and Russia, causing panic in the crowd. The outcome: 35 injured, one English fan left in a life-threatening condition. On April 6, at a time when Olympique de Marseille supporters were angry, two homemade bombs exploded near the Robert-Louis Dreyfus training center in Marseille. Supporters also waved a banner demanding the "removal" of owner Margarita Louis-Dreyfus and club president Vincent Labrune.

Football supporters had already used homemade bombs during significant violent episodes, such as a French League Cup match between Bastia and PSG in Paris in April 2015, when about 15 CRS (riot police) were wounded. In November 2015, a young steward lost two phalanges of a finger when trying to pick up a bomb thrown from the stands during a match between Lyon and Saint-Etienne in Gerland (Rhône).

The use of bombs has also been recorded:

- in November 2015, at a gathering of anti-immigration protesters in Pontivy (Morbihan).

- in October 2015, when a person was struck by a bomb during a protest at Proségur Saint-Etienne (a money transportation firm).

- at robberies, such as in November 2015, when three homemade bombs exploded and destroyed a Crédit agricole bank in Moisdon-La-Rivière (Loire-Atlantique). Three individuals were apprehended, one of whom was seriously injured 3 weeks later while tinkering with another explosive device.

Aside from terrorism, homemade bombs have been used in: urban guerilla warfare, acts of revenge, intimidation, sabotage, robberies, and vandalism, not to mention dangerous adolescent games. Thanks to several attacks that have left a lasting impression, and the ease and widespread availability of materials and bomb recipes on the Internet, explosive devices are no longer a mystery. Even the term "homemade" in this context no longer carries the implication that something is made at home, on a non-industrial scale. It now simply means something that is easy for anyone to make.

For Islamists, the attack on *Charlie Hebdo* exposed France's vulnerability. It was the start signal. A report in February 2016 by the British NGO Conflict Armament Research revealed that Daesh terrorists had produced IEDs on a large scale. About 50 companies in 20 countries, including Turkey, the United States, and the Netherlands, had produced, sold, and dispatched hundreds of constituent elements (detonators, cables, and wires) used for producing these explosive devices. The report showed that various components used for making bombs, such as aluminum powder, are not restricted in any way—for example, not subject to exportation licenses—in Turkey. And the education given to the mujahidin raises the prospect of an increase in homemade bomb attacks. In February 2014, Ibrahim B., a 23-year-old French man, was arrested just before the Carnival in Nice, where he was preparing an attack. Three tins of triacetone triperoxide were found at his home, along with a USB stick containing instructions for how to make an explosive device.

The proliferation of cases of incendiary devices being used at protests shows that these are now the preferred weapon of anarchists. But they are used more generally too:

- During the night of December 2, 2014 in Sarlat (Dordogne), a young man detonated three devices in the course of a conflict with his neighbors.

- In August 2014, 250 police officers struggled to contain fans of the football teams Bastia and Marseille. Several explosions occurred during the extremely violent clashes and 44 officers were injured.

- In July 2014, a dissatisfied customer threw explosive bottles onto a bar/tobacco counter in Darnetal (Seine-Maritime) and was only apprehended much later.

- In December 2013, the police found ingredients that could be used to make an incendiary bottle in the backpack of a 14-year-old in Allonnes (Sarthe). He admitted having caused damage on several occasions using incendiary devices, including burning a large garbage container.

- In November 2013, four students, the oldest aged 14, threw a homemade bomb into their school's gym in Montpellier.

- In July 2013, two explosive bottles were found at the Parisian home of a 14-year-old boy. His mother took him and the bomb to the police station to give an explanation.

- In March 2012, a 14-year-old arsonist threw a Molotov cocktail into a junkyard. Sixty vehicles were destroyed by the fire, causing €57,000 of damage.

- On March 21, 2012, a bomb explosion in front of the Indonesian embassy in Paris (16th arrondissement) was suspected to be a terrorist attack (unconfirmed). Nobody was injured, but the bomb destroyed everything within a fifty 50 meter radius.

- On May 30, 2011, there were three explosions in three Ikea stores in three different countries: France (Lille); Belgium (Gand); and Netherlands (Eindhoven). The blasts were weak and the damage was minimal. They were caused by booby-trapped alarm clocks hidden under pallets. Two men were apprehended in Poland: they were demanding €6 million and threatening to use more powerful bombs in other Ikea stores if they did not receive the money.

- In February 2011 in Leers (Nord), two adolescents aged 16 and 17 were seriously injured while making a homemade device.

- In October 2011 in Saint-Pol-sur-Mer (Nord), two adolescents threw four homemade bombs at police officers.

- In June 2010 near Rennes (Ille-et-Vilaine), a 15-year-old student detonated a bomb in the toilets at his school.

<u>Countries Are Reacting to the Situation</u>

Belgium is limiting the availability of explosive materials; in July 2016, the country's authorities banned the sale (until then unrestricted) of seven substances used in the production of explosive devices. According to an announcement by the ministry, these include hydrogen peroxide, which is used to produce TATP, as well as "the provision, importation, possession and use" of six other substances: nitric acid, nitromethane, and four potassium- and chlorine-based herbicides. Future regulations also include the obligation to report any suspicious transactions, losses, or thefts involving these substances and also acetone, sulfuric acid, hexamine, or sodium nitrate.

Placing these substances under surveillance strengthens the fight against terrorism. EU Regulation No 98/2013 of February 9, 2013, edition L39 of the *Official Journal of the European Union*, mandates similar restrictions. But banning a product never means eliminating it completely: weapons, drugs, and counterfeit items are easy to find everywhere. Nevertheless, it is still better to monitor these precursors than to let them circulate freely, which is too often the case nowadays.

Besides the problem of the availability of precursors, there is also the problem of their distribution. In the United Kingdom, Amazon and the bookstores WHSmith and Waterstones withdrew bomb-making manuals from their websites in November 2016. Until then, American military training handbooks from the 1960s, such as *Improvised Munitions Handbook*, *Boobytraps*, and *Explosives and Demolitions*, had been distributed through their websites by third-party publishers. It was recently revealed that such texts had also been used by criminals in the United States.

In France, also in November 2016, a municipal employee in Cannes was sentenced to 6 months in jail for having shared video tutorials about how to make homemade bombs. He had copied them from YouTube to his Facebook account.

The aggravated use of homemade devices goes hand in hand with the increase in social violence in Europe, particularly at protests connected to migration. If anarchists such as the No Border group use violence to support refugees, their opponents are no less willing to use force. In Germany, such violent actions have multiplied since the arrival of a million asylum seekers in 2015, despite a report by the German government that judged migration on that scale to be a "very serious threat to social stability and economic development."[7]

On September 26, 2016, two explosive devices were planted in Dresden, Saxony, one in front of a mosque and one on the terrace of a conference center. The second exploded about half an hour after the first. On September 25 last year, a powerful explosion in the basement of an office furniture store in Budapest wounded two police officers who were on patrol. The incident occurred shortly before the Hungarian Prime Minister held a referendum intended to validate his refusal to accept the migrants allocated to Hungary by the EU.

As France looks towards upcoming presidential and legislative elections, the question of immigration has the potential to inflame social tension even further, encouraging violence between pro- and anti-immigration groups. Violence that, in some cases, will involve homemade or incendiary bombs.

[7] *France 24*, 09/27/16

Community Safety: A Remedy for Territorial Segregation? A French Response

François Dieu[A] and Xavier Latour[B]

In France, safety is not solely a matter for the state and its police, but also involves citizens. It is constantly threatened by various social problems, especially urban segregation,[1] which seriously undermines interpersonal connections that serve as a foundation for trust, respect, and solidarity among the inhabitants of a neighborhood or city. By dividing and partitioning, such segregation instills mistrust and tension among the constituents of the population along social, religious, ethnic, and geographic lines. In addition to making it much more difficult for any action by police services, who are exposed to gang activity and mafia practices, it contributes to the development of criminal behavior. Territorial segregation, in fact, accentuates instability, resentment, and desocialization. The inhabitants of segregated areas are the first victims of greater insecurity in increasingly anomic spaces, such that some speak of them, correctly or incorrectly, using expressions such as "ghettos" and "lawless areas."[2]

State law enforcement (police and *gendarmerie*) and municipal police forces are trying to adapt by changing their methods of operation (foot patrols and neighborhood units) and organization (communities of brigades for the *gendarmerie* and priority safety areas in difficult neighborhoods). They seek to be present on the ground and reduce what is a clear division in equality between users of the public service. In spite of their efforts, the police services have, for a long time, no longer been in a position to act alone. Indeed, responses to crime, and real or felt insecurity, have become diverse, increasingly involving partnerships.[3] These include a range of methods, from situational prevention (which involves surrounding potential victims with protection by acting against situations that encourage criminal acts) to several provisions in city policies.[4] Crime prevention also involves the use of security technology such as video surveillance, now called "video protection."[5] While prevention may have

[A] Professor of Sociology at Université Toulouse 1 Capitole (CERP/IDETCOM).
[B] Professor of Public Law at Université Côte d'Azur, Faculty of Law and Political Science (Nice), Center for Studies and Research in Administrative, Constitutional, Financial, and Tax Law - Secretary General of the French Association of Security and Defense Law.

[1] Marco Oberty and Edmond Préteceille, *La Ségrégation Urbaine* (Paris: La Découverte, 2016).

[2] "Rapport 2015," Observatoire National de la Politique de la Ville, accessed April 12, 2017, www.onpv.fr/uploads/media_items/rapport-onpv-2015.original.pdf.

[3] François Dieu, *Les Réponses à la Délinquance* (Paris: L'Harmattan, 2016).

[4] Xavier Latour, "Espace urbain et délinquance, la vision du juriste," in *Le Droit de la Sécurité et de la Défense en 2014*, edited by Olivier Gohin and Bertrand Pauvert. Paris: PUAM, 2015. 343–357.

[5] François Dieu, "La sécurité à l'heure des nouvelles technologies de contrôle: l'exemple de la vidéo-surveillance," *Rivista di Criminologia, Vittimologia e Sicurezza*, 3-4(2009-10): 261–280.

a troubling catch-all aspect, and faces some skepticism concerning its effectiveness, it also includes some interesting approaches. In this regard, one of the keys to success is tackling the causes behind insecure situations, which include the loss of social reference points by one segment of the population. As emphasized in the 1983 Bonnemaison report,[6] "prevention is everyone's concern," and this is reflected in numerous provisions involving people in the construction of their own security. If they wish to protect their property and themselves against malicious acts or attacks, they have to begin by investing themselves in their immediate environment. In other words, it is up to each person to build community safety with the public authorities—as part of a kind of "security contract," by analogy with the enduring Rousseauian idea of the social contract. Community safety can be defined, on the one hand, as involving a close geographic environment (the neighborhood and the city) and, on the other hand, as being guided by the goal of reconstructing social ties. The community is both geographic and relational, and targets all forms of insecurity, from antisocial behavior to major crime.[7]

Two forms of prevention are mobilized by community safety: community prevention and social prevention, which therefore oppose the logic of urban segregation. Community prevention, which seeks to mobilize inhabitants in order to better control the social space, is reflected in four types of measures: integrating interactive spaces for inhabitants into urban planning (shops and community services, gardens and green spaces, and community centers); encouraging residents to acquire housing and develop a "sense of community" ("making neighborhoods better places to live"); implementing neighborhood councils and building neighborhood solidarity; and improving relations between the police and the population (policing by consent, and community policing).[8] Social prevention, for its part, refers to actions directed towards the potential criminal. This then involves breaking the vicious cycle that can potentially lead an individual to commit criminal acts by operating on his/her social environment. Beyond his/her individual responsibility, at a more general level, the criminal is considered as the victim of a society that has not known/been able to ensure his/her integration, and upon whom weigh factors of maladjustment and various determinisms inherent to his/her social environment, experience, and living conditions. The goal is to carry out one or several actions on the subject and his/her micro-environment (family, group of peers, and school environment), in order to reduce the risk of their committing a criminal act. In practice, leadership and employment activities intended to improve the living conditions of populations are favored in order to reverse the progress of criminality and insecurity, inexorably

[6] Gilbert Bonnemaison, and Commission des Maires sur la Sécurité (France), Face à la Délinquance: Prévention, Répression, Solidarité: Rapport au Premier Ministre (Paris: La Documentation Française, 1983).

[7] Anne Wyvekens, "Sécurité, solidarité et société civile," in Les Etats à l'Épreuve de la Sécurité, ed. Jean-Charles Froment et al. (Grenoble: Presses Universitaires de Grenoble, 2003).

[8] François Dieu, Policer la Proximité: Les Expériences Britanniques, Françaises et New Yorkaises (Paris: L'Harmattan, 2002).

linked to situations of marginalization and exclusion.

Through the convergence of legal and sociological perspectives, this article intends to provide elements that respond to the following questions, which are of acute interest in current French society: Does territorial segregation manifest itself in the issue of safety, and as a response, is it possible to develop a logic of community? In the fight against territorial segregation, what is the impact of community safety provisions, especially those involving citizen participation and social mediation? In other words, is community safety a response that is suitable (I), and effective (II), in the matter of territorial segregation?

I. Community Safety: A Suitable Response?

Territory is an important parameter for safety policies, with most notably a trend toward a measure of enclosure in administrative apportionment. The public response to crime is a prisoner of the borders imposed by the multiplicity of constituencies, both administrative (municipalities, townships, intermunicipal bodies, districts [*arrondissements*], departments [*départements*], and regions) and legal (jurisdictions of superior courts and courts of appeal). This in spite of the fact that it would be more effective to deploy police and gendarmerie forces by taking account of living areas and lines of communication, rather than enclosing them within institutional territories that are not necessarily consistent.[9] Even the level of the department, which is at the center of local policies for prevention and safety, favored by a state seeking to preserve, around the prefect, its sovereignty over safety, still does not represent a homogeneous functional territory either in terms of geography or human activities. Confronted by a criminality that is often mobile and constantly changing, the public response seems entrenched and scattered, as if hindered by narrow scopes that are extremely difficult to change, and there is a feeling that public authorities are countering dynamic phenomena with a degree of immobility. This is clearly the case when noted imbalances lead to necessary adjustments to the territorial organization of police and gendarmerie forces (A), and when it involves disseminating the logic of community safety into the ranks of these forces (B).

A) The Necessary Reform of the Police Map

The main trait of public safety policies is related to one of the primary characteristics of the French police system, namely, its dual nature, the result of the separate evolution of the rural and urban components of French society up until the beginning of the twentieth century. The police and the *gendarmerie* developed separately, one in the cities and the other in the countryside, until, under pressure from the industrial revolution and progress in communication, the rural and urban spheres

[9] Xavier Latour, "L'organisation territoriale et la sécurité intérieure," *La Semaine Juridique Administrations et Collectivités Territoriales*, 51-52 (2015): 2375.

came into contact, interaction, and conflict, to become intertwined and combined in suburban areas today. The urban concentration of populations, and as a result, safety problems, has led public authorities to favor an essentially urban perspective on insecurity. Thus, public safety policies have been primarily directed towards cities and their neighborhoods, except for a certain concern, over the last few years, for suburban areas. The public response to insecurity in rural areas has for its part adopted a traditional and pragmatic form of community police action by *gendarmerie* stations, which has led to a measure of inertia in this public action, given the sociodemographic changes in rural areas (desertification of the countryside, and suburbanization), manifested in the *gendarmerie*'s overly fixed territory-based presence.

In the matter of safety, the issue of territorial segregation has not been raised with the same intensity as in other areas of public action. In appearance, two types of territory, at the two extremes of France, seem to be the most concerned by unequal treatment: on the one hand, the disadvantaged neighborhoods in the main cities and, on the other hand, the most remote countryside areas. In spite of a measure of willingness by public authorities since the 1980s, the neighborhoods classified today as "priority regions" stand out due to an insufficient presence of public services in general, and of security services in particular. This is one of the main orientations in social urban development policies united under the scope of city policy. Since the mid-1990s, the effective integration of crime prevention as one of the priorities of city policy has caused it to become an entirely separate component of urban safety policy.[10] With regard to police organizations, the consideration of city policy objectives has been reflected (in addition to participation in crime prevention bodies) in the use of mobile forces (riot police [*Compagnies Républicaines de Sécurité*, CRS] and squadrons of mobile *gendarmerie* forces) for protection missions, by the reactivation of the practice of neighborhood units [*îlotage*] and the implementation of community policing, and by improving reception (especially of victims) at police and *gendarmerie* stations.[11] Police institutions also contribute to initiatives in crime prevention by appointing former officers as delegates of police–population cohesion [*délégués à la cohésion police-population*, DCPP] in certain difficult neighborhoods, leading "city, life, vacation" ["*ville, vie, vacances*", VVV] programs, activities for youth recreation centers [*centres de loisirs jeunes*, CLJ] by the police and juvenile crime prevention brigades [*brigades de prévention de la délinquance juvénile*, BPDJ] by the *gendarmerie*, the intervention in school environments by anti-drug police trainers [*policiers formateurs antidrogue*, PFAD] and anti-drug relay training officers [*formateurs relais antidrogue*, FRAD], as well as the appointment of representatives and advisers in the matter of school safety or the fight against domestic violence. Even though it is not a decisive factor in guiding the action of police organizations, city policy has nonetheless contributed to the dissemination of a logic of community and partnership in response to insecurity.

[10] Xavier Latour, "Espace urbain et délinquance, la vision du juriste," in *Le Droit de la Sécurité et de la Défense en 2014*, edited by Olivier Gohin and Bertrand Pauvert. (Paris: PUAM, 2015).

[11] François Dieu, Xavier Latour, and Christian Vallar (eds.), *Gendarmerie, Service Public, Service au Public* (Paris: Mare et Martin, 2017).

While the police presence is clearly insufficient in the most insecure neighborhoods in the cities, due to the breadth of problems with crime, the omnipresence of an underground economy, and the issue of gangs, as well as considerable needs for the protection and safety of the population, the situation in very rural areas is more complex. In these areas, there is certainly a sparse presence of the gendarmerie, but there is also, in spite of extremely reduced activity, the problem of the expensive upkeep of its national "grid" [*maillage*]; even while the institution does not necessarily have the human resources, it requires in suburban areas to conduct its missions, especially in community safety.

The issue was raised most notably 20 years ago by the Carraz-Hyest report (1998),[12] which sought to be the preliminary condition for major reform of the police map, often spoken about, sometimes attempted, but always sacrificed on the altar of local egotism and corporatism. And yet, the phrase used was straightforward: "The geographic distribution of the workforce of civil servants ensuring the safety of the French people is inversely proportional to the needs." By the reactions it caused, this attempt to reform the police map revealed the difficulty or even impossibility of redistributing the territories between the police and the gendarmerie. The inadequacy noted between, on the one hand, the territorial distribution of the workforce of police and gendarme officers, and, on the other hand, the changes in society and the state of crime, then led its authors to outline a redeployment made possible through the combination of two overarching developments. On the one hand, the map of the respective locations of the police and the gendarmerie was modified, and on the other hand, there was a movement towards the territorial reorganization internal to each of the two institutions, so as to free up additional personnel to strengthen their presence in sensitive neighborhoods and suburban areas. With regard to the situation of the gendarmerie and the police, the Carraz-Hyest report indicated how, in light of the differences in their organization and operation, it may be somewhat risky to make comparisons. While, aside from the extent of the space to be monitored, the situation has seemed unbalanced to the detriment of the police (with 60% of the law enforcement workforce, it is responsible for 50% of the population, 75% of criminal acts, and 80% of sensitive urban areas), the increase of the population under the gendarmerie in the matter of public safety has reduced the gap between the two institutions over the last few years. A few redeployments have nonetheless taken place in the meantime as part of a more pragmatic policy, which led to the replacement (between 2003 and 2007 in 60 departments) of gendarmerie stations by police stations in more than 200 suburban municipalities located at the edge of major cities, and of 40 police stations operating in a 100 municipalities by gendarmerie stations in medium-sized towns—fewer than 20,000 inhabitants— with a crime rate lower than the national average. Faced with the need to adjust the workforce distribution of police and gendarme officers to sociodemographic changes, successive governments have generally opted for an eas-

[12] Roland Carraz and Jean-Jacques Hyest, *Rapport au Premier ministre sur une Meilleure Répartition des Effectifs de la Police et de la Gendarmerie pour une Meilleure Sécurité Publique* (Paris: La Documentation Française, 1998).

excessive procedures that consume a large part of the operational capability, but also for a better matching of the workforce to objective needs through the gradual and ambitious reform of the police map.

Because the *gendarmerie* did not redesign the map of its stations, it was not able to fully support the movements of the population inherent to the desertification of the countryside and suburbanization. Since 2009, it has thus only been able to close 100 community stations and 40 independent stations, with the related workforce being redeployed at the local level. All of this leads us to believe that attitudes have not changed regarding the idea of the grid, which represented and still represents one of the *gendarmerie*'s pillars for development and action. Indeed, what should have followed the territorial and static concept of the grid (which corresponded to the era of the horse and bicycle) was, during the second half of the twentieth century, a more dynamic and human concept, since the referent in the matter of station location was no longer (just) the territory, but the population. In more concrete terms, and without abandoning the presence of the *gendarmerie* throughout the country, the map of its stations should have been significantly modified in order to allow for a greater concentration of resources in high-density municipalities, which would have required the closing and movement of a large number of units located in rural areas most affected by the rural exodus. There are two main arguments for redesigning the station location map: on the one hand, to preserve the principle of community for any change detrimental to the idea of *gendarmerie*, and on the other hand, to optimize the use of resources in a Malthusianism budget context. The breaking up of the gendarmerie into no less than 3,300 stations (the same number there were in the middle of the nineteenth century), even though they are now united in the nucleus of sharing that constitutes the system of station communities, participates in this antiquated and dysfunctional community approach by maintaining a territorial organization from another era.

B) The Obstacles to Community Safety

In addition to recognizing the need to reform the police map in light of the visible imbalances that negatively affect the populations of difficult neighborhoods and suburban areas, the other question to consider is whether it is possible to implement genuine community action in the matter of safety. In a pluralist democracy, the need to bring together the police and the population is uncontested, if only in reference to the very principles of public service. However, it seem to be very difficult in France to establish this mindset in a sustainable way for the generation of safety, in spite of the progress made over the last few years in partnerships and prevention policies. In reality, there seem to be at least three related trends that stand in the way of community safety, which remains up to the state to draft and design: the primacy of individualism, the state control of safety, and the ambivalent relationship to law and order.

As a process by which the individual is liberated from the rules and values of the collective consciousness, individualism postulates the individual's independence from collective rules and his/her liberation from the norms imposed by others; in other words, the traditional protections that weigh on his/her existence. Originally, individualism was indistinguishable from the ideas of modernity and democracy shaped by the philosophy of the Enlightenment, before then being associated—as it became more generally accepted in the second half of the twentieth century—with a crisis in citizenship and sociability, and even with a setback in the logic of solidarity and the permissiveness of postmodern society. It has become commonplace to emphasize the constant progress of this individualism in social relations, which tends to further stretch relations between individuals, all the more when it involves relationships that each person maintains with representatives of law enforcement. This erosion can thus be seen in the exercise of the *gendarmerie*'s mission of general surveillance.[13]

In France, safety is based on a state logic such that public authorities, even though they authorize the invaluable support of municipalities and their groupings as well as the private sector, nonetheless maintain a genuine monopoly that is exercised by the executive power. The corollary of this state control is the preponderance of police responses produced by the two sovereign institutions (the police and the *gendarmerie*), both of which are national and under the responsibility of the Ministry of the Interior. Thus, French police is a state police, that is, under the exclusive authority of the central (executive) power, as well as a police of law and order with the priority to maintain public order. This fundamentally sovereign and police-based dimension to safety is no doubt an obstacle to the emergence of a logic of community policing.

This model covers the experiences intended to strengthen the visibility of police action and communication between the police and the population. As a way of managing public safety, it does not negate the ultimately coercive nature of the police function. It is a particular position adopted by the police organization characterized by a concern to establish partnerships with various social actors in order to carry out security-related tasks, the legitimacy of which can, furthermore, only be strengthened by the coming together of police officers and citizens. Based on a community approach to social relations, this form of "gentle" and "proactive" police has three characteristics. First, it is decentralized and recognizes the significant practical independence of departments and agents. Second, it is accepted by the population and encourages persuasion and prevention, and communication and collaboration with the public, thanks to an increase in police presence on the ground and the implementation of situational prevention mechanisms. Finally, it is based on an expansive view of the police mandate. It supposes, on the one hand, the involvement of police departments in resolving problems through the collective search for common factors in a series of disturbances in order to enable a non-sequential response. On the other hand, it allows for police priorities to be adapted to citizen expectations, with the implementation of surveys that make it possible to understand population expectations and evaluate police action. While the idea of community policing seems somewhat attractive, as long

[13] François Dieu, Sécurité et Proximité. La Mission de Surveillance Générale de la Gendarmerie (Paris: L'Harmattan, 2002).

as it is part of an integrated view of police work that conforms to a pluralist ideology, it seems difficult to implement for police institutions that are based (as in France) on authoritarian and centralized mindsets, which have endured beyond the arrival of the Republican regime. While for the *gendarmerie* we can speak, empirically, of age-old community police (which, however, is currently somewhat eroding), for the national police, traditional police practices (neighborhood police) were, between 1997 and 2002, subject to an attempt at institutionalization that was confronted by cultural resistance, organizational constraints, and ideological differences.

Evolving in a social context dominated by individualism as the producer of safety geared primarily toward the protection of the state, its sovereignty, and public order, the French police officer has experienced chronic mistrust, and even an aversion to the organization, on the part of the population, which can be explained, in large part, by the weight of history and popular representations. The police officer is first the easy victim, catalyst, and scapegoat for the ambiguous relationship of the French people with order and public power. This questioning of the state apparatus's intention is a constant in western countries fed by a liberal ideology, but it is even more significant in countries like France that are characterized by a national political history marked by numerous episodes of political violence. The arrival of democracy remains in France a recent event, after several centuries of oppressive power and its traumatizing return in the twentieth century under the Vichy regime. Thus, the French, even though today they live in a stable democracy, have more or less consciously maintained a degree of mistrust towards state power, which is inevitably suspected, in the collective imagination, of plotting against their individual liberties.

The relationship to law and order is undermined by this trait in the French political culture. To summarize, due to its inability to leave behind this collective psychosis, France has an ambiguous relationship with its police, which is not limited (far from it) to the troubled relationship with the youth of difficult neighborhoods. The problem is much broader even though it is only marginally manifested by direct confrontations. The French are wary of law and order and thus of their police, even though the police benefit from a high level of trust that is very respectable among the population (*gendarme* and police officers received, respectively, a positive opinion rating of 81% and 65% in an IFOP poll taken in November 2014 for *L'Essor de la Gendarmerie Nationale*) and, to a lesser degree, among young people (52% of high schoolers expressed this trust in the police, compared to 85% for the army, in the *Enquête sur les Jeunes et les Armées* conducted in 2011 by IRSEM, the Institute of Strategic Research of the Military School). Another survey, conducted for *L'Express* (February 11 –17, 2015), admittedly a few weeks after the attacks of January 2015, and after expressions of sympathy for police and *gendarme* officers especially during the demonstration on January 11 (which even led the singer Renaud to "hug a cop" in one of his recent compositions), indicated that 84% of the French appear to have a positive opinion of police officers (17% a very positive opinion and 67% a fairly positive opinion). These quantified opinions surely reveal very important expectations in the matter of security, which justifies control measures that, for their part, are far from popular. This ambivalence in the relationship to law and order is one of the many determinants in the production of safety. It undermines the relationship of the citizen with the police, by placing the latter and its agents in a kind of schizophrenic situation, and thus impedes the potential emergence of the logic of community safety.

II) Community Safety: An Effective Response?

As part of a logic of prevention that does not exclusively involve the police, community safety can adopt different provisions, such as citizen participation (A) and social mediation (B). These provisions reveal ambiguities in community safety: valued in the sense that it seeks to encourage social mobilization and a preventive response to crime, it nonetheless calls into question the material and symbolic monopoly of the public authorities and their police. Accompanied by limits and reservations, it struggles to be applied and demonstrate its effectiveness, in spite of often encouraging early results.

A) Community Safety and Citizen Participation

Well-known through Anglo-American "neighborhood watch" provisions,[14] community safety was popularized in France through "vigilant neighbors," an experiment from 10 years ago in the Alpes-Maritimes region. The principle, based on a partnership between security forces and inhabitants, has two advantages. On one hand, it brings together police officers and inhabitants in a neighborhood. Actions are structured around a network that feeds information to the police, while also sending out rules and prevention advice to the population. On the other hand, a social link is recreated between people motivated by the desire to serve the group. Confronted by urban segregation, citizen participation contributes to revitalizing the social fabric, with the inhabitants coming together for a common goal: their safety. They are formed into a network of contact persons for police forces. Citizens are called upon to be a part of a mission to monitor their usual area of living. Better than anyone, they are the eyes and ears of what is around them: they are able to identify suspicious behavior and events, and then pass that information on to the police.

After a few years of experimenting with a solution promoted initially to improve the fight against burglaries, a few cities, in the aftermath of the terrorist attacks in November 2015, created provisions that appealed to the civic engagement of inhabitants, by extending mobilization to attack prevention. Although each local initiative is unique, the participation of citizens in their safety is neither novel nor problematic in principle. In concrete terms, inhabitants are made aware of safety issues and participate directly in a form of social control based on civic engagement and the community. Neighborhoods become active, and new ties cause individualism to recede.

[14] François Dieu, "La police de proximité en Angleterre: un bilan mitigé," Les Cahiers de la Sécurité Intérieure, 39 (2000): 123–148.

This monitoring is intended not only to supplement the police, but also to improve the prevention of antisocial behavior, and lead to a reduction in objective or felt insecurity. To accomplish this, security forces and mayors rely on a more or less developed network of associations (neighborhood associations, for example), in a logic of partnership.

The interest expressed by some municipalities in citizen participation led the *gendarmerie* to set up, centrally, a "partnerships and prevention bureau," while the police opted for a "prevention and cooperation safety advisor." Locally since 2007, the police and *gendarmerie* "safety referrers" have played an active role in this regard, beyond their involvement in consulting assignments concerning video surveillance and protection of public buildings. Several aspects of social life are involved. In parallel with burglary prevention, more targeted networks directly involve professions with the support of the local bodies concerned (industry, business, agriculture, and even sometimes professional associations), while road safety makes use, for example, of retirees as crossing guards ("yellow vests"). More recently, communication technology has been integrated into the operations of citizen networks, as soon as it is appropriate to alert a particular segment of the population concerning a danger. As part of this appeal to the population, we can include the development of the very effective provision of "kidnapping alerts."

Citizen participation refers to a range of procedures that go beyond the experiments of "vigilant neighbors," a name that was also used commercially (voisinsvigilants.org) and suffers from a negative image. The mayor is the hub for citizen participation, which requires that he/she adhere to it and be involved, before any agreement with the prefecture is signed. A large number of mayors are still somewhat reticent to become part of this kind of provision, often due to ignorance or over-cautiousness. In its area of competence, the *gendarmerie* has been particularly involved in the development of citizen participation, especially in putting in place the necessary community informing for mayors. If the mayor is willing to implement this provision, the *gendarmerie* first intervenes (as a force for advice and proposals) to identify problems, determine the geographic area (a neighborhood, housing estate, etc.), and appoint referrers (volunteers and people known in their neighborhoods who are available and present, who have good relations with city hall, and are generally comfortable in relationships with others). Generally, the referrers appointed by the mayor benefit from an initial training meeting (supplied by the *gendarmerie*), in addition to a visit to the *gendarmerie*'s operational center [*centre opérationnel de la gendarmerie*, CORG], with the possibility of meeting once a year to receive some retraining.

Except for notices indicating the provision, citizen participation produces no notable changes in the life of the neighborhoods concerned: it does not lead to the organization of self-defense patrols or the implementation of private security services, but seeks only to accentuate vigilant actions and develop more effective behaviors in terms of alerting and communicating with the *gendarmerie* and the municipal police, with referrers being given greater responsibility. It thus does not involve disturbing the normal life of the neighborhood, but is simply a matter of paying a little more attention and communicating more systematically and quickly with the *gendarmerie* station. In no way should referrers intervene to conduct verifications or other checks, and their priority remains burglary prevention.

Although there has been no long-term evaluation of what remains a recent policy applied differently depending on the municipality, these provisions tend to restore a climate of safety and serve as a deterrent for some burglars. They can thus strengthen the connection between neighbors, help the integration of new arrivals, and encourage initiatives for neighborhood life. In spite of their current popularity, the real impact on the level of crime is far from clear. The difficulty of maintaining a provision over the long term also needs to be considered. The involvement of members of the network can wane and the mobilization of new inhabitants is not always easy. Collaboration also depends on the involvement of police and *gendarmerie* forces, especially with regard to how network meetings are conducted. More practically, and in response to those who are most skeptical, no major problems have been noted, which would have no doubt led to a great deal of media coverage. In spite of these benefits, citizen participation is not a miracle provision, able to make burglaries disappear all by itself, but instead an additional tool in crime prevention, similar to patrols, video surveillance cameras, and home protection measures. It should thus be included in the spectrum of prevention tools available to the mayor, with the advantage of giving the population a role, making it responsible, and raising its status.

Citizen participation can also adopt other forms, related more generally to community prevention. These include social watch provisions, which enable the collection of information regarding problems of insecurity and exclusion, as well as abuse and crime, especially of vulnerable persons (children, spouses, and the elderly); volunteer visits to the elderly, particularly to prevent the exploitation of weakness by those around them or by dishonest persons; neighborhood meetings with the population, either periodically or after a significant event occurs (these meetings allow for direct exchange and to quickly pass on information, and may serve as a starting point for the implementation of a citizen participation provision); warning networks for shop owners and mayors ("Vigicommerces" and "Vigimaires"), which allow the *gendarmerie* or police to instantly send operational or prevention messages at the departmental level by taking advantage of current communication tools (SMS and email); monitoring and exchange provisions concerning citizenship and public peace, discussion forums for actors on the ground with the goal of promoting shared diagnostics of crime problems and encouraging the exchange of responses offered.

These various actions are not developed without a legal framework. In this regard, a circular dated June 22, 2011 dedicated to citizen participation specified the conditions under which "partnership actions" were to be carried out. Urban spaces are of course targeted, as well as rural areas. Participants are volunteers that have no legal prerogatives. The network is created based on a three-part agreement partnering the municipality, the prefect, and the police or *gendarmerie* forces. Either way, the state seeks to maintain control of citizen participation and make it work in strict compliance with the provisions of the French Internal Safety Code [*Code de la Sécurité*

Intérieure, CSI] and the General Local Authorities Code [*Code Général des Collectivités Territoriales*, CGCT]. Indeed, it is up to the state to ensure safety based on article L 111-1 CSI, which calls upon the prefect to lead and coordinate the internal safety provision (article L 122-1 CSI). He/She acts in close contact with the mayor, the hub for crime prevention in the municipality (article L 132-2 CSI). As a result, by associating inhabitants with the work of the security forces, citizen participation has to be part of this three-way relationship.

Informant or community-spirited? This dilemma is often raised when it comes to organizing citizen participation in safety in general, and that of municipalities in particular. In France, the results of the solution have, moreover, been rather mixed: 1,260 municipalities adopted it in gendarmerie areas compared to only 60 in police areas.[15] The announcement of the first results in certain municipalities in the North and Alpes-Maritimes was accompanied by a flurry of criticism, some of which compared it with the "citizen rounds" initiated in Italy by the Northern League, while others emphasized the impossibility of transposing a system that was too Anglo-American. The top prize, as it were, went to a website (http://probe.20minutes-blogs.fr/archive/2010/03/15/operation-voisins-vigilants.html) that illustrated a few articles on the topic with photos taken from the film by Yves Boisset, *Dupont Lajoie* (1975), showing the rape scene of a teenage girl and the lynching of a North African worker suspected of having committed the crime. However, citizen participation does not involve being paid for informing the police of criminal acts, as it does in South Korea, but is instead meant to provide valuable assistance to police officers and *gendarmes*. While citizen participation in crime prevention is a matter of civic engagement and co-production of safety, it must still be done in compliance with the law.

The administrative tribunal of Montpellier reiterated this in an interim order of January 19, 2016, then in a judgment on the merits, July 5, 2016,[16] involving the "Beziers guard" project initiated by a mayor, which was controversial and received wide media attention. Based on a resolution by the municipal council on December 15, 2015, the city of Beziers decided to create a "Beziers guard" responsible for supporting law enforcement. By appealing to retirees from the police and the *gendarmerie*, the city sought to benefit from volunteer reinforcements intended to have "guards in place in front of public buildings and walk-abouts on public roads." In no case were these citizens to act; on the contrary, they were only supposed to alert law enforcement if there was a problem. This decision, clearly taken without consulting the Hérault prefecture, received a lot of media attention and raised the ire of the local prefect. Calming the debate between the proponents of civic engagement and those who feared the creation of a militia, he submitted a request to the administrative judge for a summary suspension (article L 544-1 of the French Code of Administrative Jus-

[15] Written question No. 27672 of May 28, 2013, OJ response November 11, 2014, p. 9516.

[16] Tribunal Administratif de Montpellier, July 5, 2016, No. 1506696; "Il n'y aura pas de garde biterroise", *L'Actualité Juridique Droit Administratif*, July 11, 2016, 1368; *JCPA* 2016, 2250; note from Xavier Latour.

tice), and a claim of annulment. In an order dated January 19, 2016, the judge decided to suspend the municipal council's resolution due to "serious doubt" regarding its legality, a doubt confirmed in substance. The city of Beziers sought first to justify the creation of its "guard" by referring to the notion of occasional collaborator with the public service. While, in terms of media coverage, it could have compared it to the "vigilant neighbors" provision, the municipality did not take up this argument with the judge.

It is true that citizen participation depends on a partnership between municipalities and state actors in safety, namely, the prefect and police forces. While it has value in making the population aware of crime prevention, it is not in any way comparable with the Beziers version, which was much more extensive, and involved actions usually carried out by private security (building guards), and police services (monitoring of public roads). The reference to occasional collaborator with the public service was, in any case, not very convincing. Applied in the matter of administrative responsibility, this supposes that an individual outside of the public service can be called upon to participate in it, either at the request of the service, or in a spontaneous way. If he/she acts at the request of the service, it must be justified by a particular need. If he/she acts spontaneously, it must be in response to an emergency. In this particular case, reference to collaborators was insufficient to use as a basis for the ruling. The judge in chambers found, setting aside the argument for exceptional circumstances that were neither established or even mentioned, that the municipal council, "*based on any legislative or regulatory provision currently in effect, was not competent to create, at its own initiative and for an undetermined length of time, an operational service with a view to conferring to individuals, appointed or designated by the mayor as occasional collaborators with the public service, missions to monitor public roads or buildings which, in municipalities, are the concern of the municipal police and are conducted . . . by the mayor or by agents placed under his/her authority and under the control of the representative of the state.*"

It was hard to find a more solid element among the arguments the city presented to the judge. This was no doubt a sign that there was no better argument, except perhaps that anything that is not explicitly prohibited is permitted. Established constitutional (CW 2011-625 of March 10, 2011) and administrative (CS, Ass. June 17, 1932 City of Castelnaudary) case law shows to what degree public authorities maintain a monopoly in the matter of safety.[17] For comparison, if private security acts alongside law enforcement, it does so within a limited scope, which does not allow it, in principle, to monitor public roads. As specified by the administrative tribunal in

[17] Xavier Latour and Pierre Moreau, "Délégation et activités de police: stop ou encore?", *La Semaine Juridique Administrations et Collectivités Territoriales*, 15 (2012): 41-44; Elina Lemaire, "Actualité du principe de prohibition de la privatisation de la police," *Revue Française de Droit Administratif*, 4 (2009): 767; Jacques Petit, "Nouvelles d'une antinomie: contrat et police," in *Mélanges en l'Honneur de Jacques Moreau*. (Paris: Éditions Economica, 2003). 345; Gabriel Eckert, "Police et contrat," in *La Police Administrative*, edited by Charles Vautrot-Schwarz (Paris: Presses universitaires de France, 2014), 167.

a well-argued recital, neither the Internal Security Code (CSI) nor the General Local Authorities Code (CGCT) provides a legal basis for the city's decision. So what about an initiative that comes from the citizens themselves? In accordance with article L 111-1 CSI, the state has "*the duty to ensure safety by attending, for the entirety of the territory of the Republic, to the defense of national institutions and interests in compliance with the laws, to the maintenance of public peace and order, to the protection of persons and property.*" This explains the automatic participation of the prefect in citizen participation provisions, which confirms article L 122-1 according to which he "*leads and coordinates the entirety of the provision of internal security.*" Certainly, the mayor "*contributes to the crime prevention policy*" (article L 2211-1 CGCT), but only in compliance with state law and the hierarchy of norms. Is the duty of the prefect and the participation of the mayor enough to prevent volunteering that complies with the rules of engagement?

Aside from the controversy, the creation of the "Beziers guard" should not mask a fundamental debate. Real or supposed insecurity combined with a state discourse focused on participation encourages a variety of initiatives. In this regard, would it not be judicious to begin by disassociating public buildings from public roads? In buildings placed under the sole responsibility of the municipality, is the decision's illegality so clear? Just as a municipality is able to confer monitoring to a private security company, why should it not be able to grant it to volunteer citizens, related to it by an agreement? How would such an approach threaten the role of the state in the matter of safety? In this area, it would be better to have talks with local unions rather than the prefect. The situation is different on public roads since these are the primary area of police forces. However, citizens are already on public roads, often in coordination with the municipal police as part of road safety after school. Following the attacks of 2015, municipalities mobilized "vigilant citizens" and volunteers to monitor areas around schools. Just within Alpes-Maritimes, Saint-Laurent du Var, Cannes, Nice, and Villeneuve-Loubet, they were used without raising the ire of the prefecture. Perhaps by looking to experiences in other countries and coordinating with state representatives, would it not be possible for changes to be made? It bears recalling that any citizen can make use of article 73 of the Code of Criminal Procedure to intervene in the case of a blatant offense or crime and that he/she must, in addition, provide assistance to a person in danger. Each person is thus, in his/her own way, a monitor of the public roads. Even communication technology may shift the lines. The number of networked applications that alert citizens and/or law enforcement is growing, with increasingly greater capabilities. This causes citizens to organize and reappropriate the monitoring of public roads, without a desire to compete with the state, but only out of a concern to repair the relationships of solidarity in a context of declared "war" against terrorism.

What still needs to be determined is how to structure these initiatives to make them truly useful and legally acceptable. The assessment of the successes and failures of citizen participation cannot only involve a numbers-based approach to crime. It can affecimpact the perceptions of the population by police forces and vice- versa.

Civic engagement is also a Republican value worth encouraging. Citizen participation should thus not be condemned a priori. It all depends on the framework in which it is carried out, and the amount of room to maneuver granted to participants. This limited room to maneuver for citizen participation is, conversely, greater in the case of social mediation, which is nonetheless just as problematic.

B) Community Safety and Social Mediation

In many situations, local authorities, public institutions for intermunicipal co-operation, social landlords, and carriers can rely on associations to develop provisions in order to defuse conflicts, soothe tensions, and develop the feeling of safety.[18] All are reassured by a method focused on "the idealization of social relationships."[19] This social mediation, which falls under social prevention, is consensual enough to transcend political divides. Mediators are present, for example, in front of schools, on public transport,[20] and in certain neighborhoods. These local social mediation agents work under different titles (night contacts, mediation agents, etc.), but they are all players in social regulation.[21] Mobilized for the fight against antisocial behavior, these mediators also take action against petty crime, by involving affected parties in the process of resolution and prevention. They generally benefit from a good knowledge of the area in which they operate and the populations they meet.

Social mediation has gradually become an entirely separate profession, with its rules and organizations. The desire to break with practices that were not rigorous and even counterproductive has been clearly affirmed. The recruitment of disreputable and poorly trained people degraded the image of this form of prevention. After years of mistakes due to the lack of a regulatory framework (unlike penal or family mediation), the trend is being reversed. At the beginning of the 2000s, the law concerning social mediation became more specific in terms of safety, on the one hand, and in terms of city and welfare policy, on the other. Social mediation was first the topic of circulars at the end of the 1990s (October 28 and December 15, 1997). Social mediation mechanisms were addressed in the environment of local safety contracts [*contrats locaux de sécurité*, CLS], and the assessments that accompanied them. While the law of March 18, 2001 on internal security made social mediation a focus of safety policy, the law of August 1, 2003 on orientation and programming for the city and urban renewal tackled it from another, complementary, angle. Two objectives for the same method. At best, this can be perceived from the perspective of complementarity;

---

[18] Jacques de Maillard, "Des médiateurs locaux pour améliorer la sécurité," in *Réformer la Police et la Sécurité*, edited by Sebastien Roché (Paris: Odile Jacob, 2004), 189–210.

[19] Fathi Ben Mrad, "La médiation sociale: entre résolution des conflits et sécurité urbaine," *Revue Française des Affaires Sociales*, 3 (2004): 232.

[20] Damien Collard, "Une déviance à double tranchant, entre désordres et innovations, le cas des agents d'ambiance de la SNCF," *Annales des Mines – Gérer et Comprendre*, 3 (2011): 8–16.

[21] Tanguy Le Goff, "L'insécurité 'saisie' par les maires. Un enjeu de politiques municipales," *Revue Française de Science Politique*, 3 (2005): 415–444.

at worst, the two objectives can be seen as competing with one other or indeterminate. The "Equality and Citizenship" bill (tabled April 13, 2016) did not really settle this issue. Of course, social mediation cannot be disassociated, according to the promoters of the document, from real equality. However, it is expected to pass through the new citizen reserve of the national police (new articles L 411-18 to 22 CSI) to promote it.

Concomitantly, or almost, local civil service law includes the logic of social mediation. This logic reunites the line of "leadership" with the decree of April 30, 2002. To encourage access to jobs in category C or B, a third contest has been opened up. It is available to persons able to demonstrate at least 4 years of professional experience related to the assignments in the range of jobs (decree of May 3, 2002). Immediate integration into local public service is not the only way to enter social mediation. Under a policy of positive discrimination, the mediators recruited can be young people that have benefited from contracts signed as part of the paths of access to civil service jobs [*parcours d'accès aux fonctions publiques*, PACTE, order of August 2, 2005]. In this way, the state uses the relay of communities to facilitate access to stable jobs, while also renewing the social environment of local civil service. In 2011, social mediation was recognized by the Interministerial Committee for Towns [*Comité Interministériel des Villes*, CIV of February 18, 2011]. The decree of October 11, 2012 supplemented "the description of assignments of local deputy moderators and local moderators when they intervene in the area of social mediation." From return to work assistance (or for access to employment in social work especially) for troubled youth (71% have a level lower than a high-school diploma in public land transport)[22] to prevention of antisocial behavior, social mediation mobilizes various resources. While volunteering plays a part, promoters access jobs supported by the state (47% in public land transport). These jobs, regardless of what they are called, come in to replace local subsidies often given to intermediary associations. In this way, a financially dependent link is created between local safety policy and the national public policy for employment, a dependence on the state strengthened by the granting of sums awarded by the interministerial fund for crime prevention [*fonds interministériel de prévention de la délinquance*, FIPD].

While the law has entered into the realm of social mediation, it remains, in principle, separate from its actions. The particularity of mediation is in fact that it does not mobilize legal prerogatives, because it is disconnected from a repressive and, more generally, police-oriented mindset. It relies, conversely, on the accountability of the affected parties. However, mediators are usually integrated into safety partnership provisions. Their action falls under local safety strategies, even though they participate in local and intermunicipal councils for safety and crime prevention [*conseils locaux et intercommunaux de sécurité et de prévention de la délinquance,* CLSPD, CISPD].

---

[22] La Médiation Sociale dans les Transports Publics Terrestres: État des Lieux 2014", Ministère de l'Écologie, du Développement Durable, et de l'Énergie, accessed April 12, 2017, http://www.france-mediation.fr/images/lang/fr/orki/mediation_sociale_transports_etat_des_lieux.pdf.

Questions are sometimes raised concerning the profile of the persons recruited and their effectiveness. It is a delicate affair to separate the effects of mediation from those resulting from other methods. The framework for intervention by associations can therefore be compared to that of private security companies. The persons recruited are not subject to the same administrative checks on morality and competence as private agents. Furthermore, does the use of associations not lead to a kind of unfair competition? In this regard, the case law of the Council of State does not really help to clarify the situation.[23] However, associations have developed the habit of intervening in parallel or in place of private security companies. They do so generally without submitting to the provisions of this code, on the pretext that they are apparently involved in mediation, not safety. The issue of not-for-profit activities is, however, subject to debate. While article L. 611-1 refers only to "services," without being any more specific, the rest of Book VI only concerns companies. There is, therefore, a legal void that needs to be filled. It would be paradoxical, on the one hand, for volunteers not to be checked, even though they conduct assignments that are identical to commercial service providers, and, on the other hand, to allow unfair competition to continue in spite of the advantage this could represent, especially in the life of small municipalities (garage sales, fairs, etc.). Clarification is even more necessary due to the fact that certain contracts are granted to mediation associations that carry out assignments often very similar to private security activities.

On this matter, the case law has led to questionable results. For example, the night mediation services that were subject to a contractual injunction were not, in this case, compared to private security activities. The judge noted that mediators' activity, for the whole territory of the municipality, involved ensuring a presence that is intended, overall, to maintain and strengthen relations with and between inhabitants, prevent and alleviate conflicts that may arise, and report, if necessary, any disruption to the public order to the relevant authorities, especially law enforcement, the only ones responsible for ensuring public order and peace. Even though this activity includes identifying problems that may affect the buildings of some landlords, the judge held that the night mediation services were seeking neither to ensure the monitoring or security of specifically identified movable or immovable property, nor to ensure the safety of persons found in these buildings. Thereupon, considering that these services came under monitoring or security activities described in section No. 1 of article L. 611-1 CSI, the interim injunction judge inaccurately qualified the facts. Thereafter, there was no basis to support that the execution of the services subject to the contract could only be done, in application of articles L. 612-1 and L. 612-6 CSI, by a natural or legal person registered with the trade and companies register and having authorization.

This assessment was particularly surprising, because if mediators are not responsible for the monitoring of buildings; this means, on the contrary, that they are appointed to the monitoring of public roads, which the judge recognized, moreover,

[23] CS ord. March 27, 2015, No. 386862.

by emphasizing that they could alert law enforcement. Yet, the monitoring of public roads is precisely part of the administrative police's operations that cannot be delegated. Was this decision not then reflective of the administrative judge's awkward position? By keeping mediation separate from checks, he did not risk destabilizing the balance of a system that rests on flexible recruitment. Who would stand to gain by introducing limitations and thus costs? It is easier to pull mediation to the social side than to the side of safety. Employers thus have the desired room to maneuver to use this lever of social peace.

In conclusion, in spite of some reticence regarding law enforcement and their perceived ineffectiveness in the struggle against daily petty crime, the French people prefer trusting them to any kind of intervention by volunteer citizens and volunteers that aims to promote, under rigorous oversight by police services, reflexes of vigilance and solidarity similar to those encountered, for the most destitute, in humanitarian associations and movements. These reservations also apply to social mediation, here again in spite of a healthy social voluntarism.

Community safety nonetheless represents a promising part of the response to crime, along with the strengthening of protection measures, which will be capable of producing significant results in the matter of security, but also and especially in strengthening social ties and community solidarity. In summary, this secondary, even marginal place for citizens in safety policies is also seen in the minimal attention paid to the population in analyzing crime, especially in local safety assessments, with the almost total absence of public meetings and the paltry successes of victimization surveys, in an area largely dominated by police statistics in spite of their limits and instrumentalization. When it comes to promoting the community, it is very much therefore a case of introducing more citizenship, and thus perhaps more democracy, into safety.

Improving Prevention and Protection against Terrorism and Other Criminal Attacks on Schools and Educational Institutions

Raymond H.A. Carter[A]

Introduction

Today international terrorism directly or indirectly affects almost every part of our world, in various forms of dangerous blind aggression directed against populations of all ages in the countries concerned, those who pass through them, and their property. These attacks are most often perpetrated by a minority who takes advantage of "democratic freedoms" in order to carry out crimes resulting in the death of innocent victims who are ill-equipped or simply helpless to deal with them. Although this phenomenon is not entirely new, it is nonetheless a real threat to the equilibrium of our nations and to their future, at the level of the state, that of businesses, and that of citizens who welcome "migrants" into their homelands today. The primary aim of "terrorism" remains "the destabilization of society through violence and fear." What is more, as we have indicated elsewhere, organized crime is increasingly "flirting" with terrorism in the sphere of "narco-terrorism" and even that of "war crimes and crimes against humanity."[1]

[A] Colonel (retired) of the Gendarmerie Nationale, Doctor in public law and international penal law, Professor of International Criminal Law at the Centre d'Études Diplomatiques et Stratégiques (C.E.D.S.), Paris, and associate professor at several universities; he is also a nationally-qualified teacher in aquatic and swimming technique and in martial arts, and serves as an expert in the European Commission on the war against terrorism and international crime. He is the author of over twenty books. A Chevalier de la Legion d'Honneur, he is also an Officier des Palmes Académiques and recipient of the Médaille d'or de la Jeunesse et des Sports.

[1] See Raymond H.A. Carter, "La triangulaire du crime," in *Le Tribunal Pénal International pour l'Ex-Yougoslavie* (Paris: L'Harmattan, 2004); "Justice Pénale Internationale et 'criminel de guerre'," in *Revue Enjeux diplomatiques et stratégiques*—2016 (Paris: C.E.D.S.), 95–105; "La Piraterie Maritime: à la fois 'Brigandage' et 'Terrorisme Maritime' dans le Golfe de Guinée et notamment en Côte d'Ivoire," *Fraternité Matin* (Côte d'Ivoire), January 2013; *La Sûreté des Transports* (Paris Presses Universitaires de France, 2008).

1. The General Context and the French Situation

These attacks have hit many countries,[2] and France is no exception, the most notable case being the attacks of November 13, 2015, which caused at least 129 deaths, many of them in the Bataclan theatre—an attack for which the terrorist group Islamic State (Daesh) claimed the responsibility. They are often perpetrated by means of a series of shootings and suicide bombings carried out with a vehicle and/or on foot. We now know that even "schools" constitute targets for these absolutely cowardly criminal acts. A counter-offensive is unavoidable if we are to deal with the situation and succeed in establishing the adequate "cooperation," genuine "collaboration," and "coordination" that goes beyond mere lip service and moves forward to mitigate this "evil," putting in place specific systems and appropriate information and training. One thing is certain: this terrorism is driven by the credo of a "global caliphate"; so we are all involved, and must react. For, as General De Gaulle said, either "the irresponsibility of intellect" must end, or "there will no longer be a West."[3]

2. A "Sensitive" Target Imperative to Take into Account: "Schools"

The threat against educational institutions in France is a known one, and it is not new. Let us recall right away the May 15, 1993 attack on the Commandant-Charcot elementary school in Neuilly-sur-Seine, where my friend Daniel Boulanger, then head of an intervention team of the anti-terrorist RAID unit, and to whom we pay tribute here, neutralized a man who was still holding six of the 21 children he had taken hostage 46 hours previously;[4] or the attack on the Ozar Hatorah Jewish high school in Toulouse on March 19, 2012, when a man wearing a video camera on his bloodied chest arrived in front of the school on a motorbike and immediately opened fire in the direction of the school yard, killing a teacher attempting to protect his two 3 and 6 year-old sons, who were also killed. The attack claimed four victims in total. Further substantiation of this threat against "the school" comes from Daesh

---

2. On March 22, 2016 in Brussels (Belgium), and March 13, 2016 in Bassam (Côte d'Ivoire), for instance. And once again on December 16, 2014 in Pakistan, where a group of Taliban insurgents from the Tehreek-e-Taliban (TTP) group, six in number, attacked a school in Peshawar in the north-west of the country, killing 141 people including 132 children, during an assault which lasted almost seven hours and also left all the attackers dead, one from detonating a bomb he was wearing. This was the bloodiest terrorist attack in Pakistan's history. In fact, a military doctor gave a course in emergency first aid when the attackers arrived at the back of the school and began to open fire; and one student who escaped the attack stated that the teachers had locked the door, that they were all lying on the ground, but that the militants broke down the door, fired into the air before aiming at the students, and left quickly afterwards.

3 Cited in André Malraux, *Fallen Oaks: Conversation with De Gaulle*, trans. Irene Clephane (London: Hamilton, 1972), 30–31.

4 Following a lengthy judicial investigation, the court concluded in favor of Boulanger, who had opened fire on Erick Schmitt, alias the "Human Bomb."

itself, who clearly announced it just after the attacks of November 13, 2015, in its French propaganda magazine *Dar al-Islam*.[5] The magazine issued a call to arms against a French school, which it presented as "the antechamber to Hell." In France we have some 63,600 schools and other educational institutions (under the patronage of the Ministry of National Education, Higher Education, and Research [*Ministère de l'Éducation nationale, de l'Enseignement supérieur et de la Recherche*, MENESR]), 54,800 public sectors and 8,800 private sectors, including 52,200 schools, 7,100 colleges, 1,600 technical colleges, and 2,700 other (LEGT, LPO, and EREA) colleges, these institutions representing a total of 12,775,400 students and apprentices.[6] In order to To confront the state of affairs outlined above, the French Government has taken specific measures.

3. National Directives

Following the 2015 attacks, and seeking to reassure the parents of these 12,775,400 students, after a first progress report presented on January 13, 2017 by Mme Najat Vallaud-Belkacem, the French Government, via the MENESR together with the Ministry of the Interior, announced measures for prevention and security in schools, high schools, and colleges to protect students, teachers, and personnel. Devised in consultations with staff organizations, representatives of Catholic education, and local authorities, the points on the governmental plan, a ministerial source revealed, revolve around "three watchwords": "Anticipate; Secure; Know how to react."

The first element of "anticipation" was set in order to involve the "training of the trainers" expected to be in place by the end of June 2017 (220 extra academic trainers in addition to 80 trainers for the regional education authorities for the beginning of the 2017–2018 school year), who will be trained in the centers of the Gendarmerie Nationale. They will be responsible for providing crisis management training for school directors from the beginning of the same school year. This should allow for a threefold increase in staff with such training (from 500 to 1,500 school principals, etc., in 2017–2018). Secondly, in order to ensure a stronger coordination

[5] This magazine, which exists to promote the "Islamic State" created in 2014, is available online in France, as is Dabiq, the English magazine of Islamic State; both are products of the mysterious multimedia agency Al-Hayat, and constitute the organ of communication of Daesh, diffusing its propaganda on Twitter. The authors rejoice in being "the witnesses of a new era," that of the restoration of the caliphate, finally allowing Muslims to live in accordance with Islamic law. The anonymous authors of the articles contained in them also denounce the "idolaters"—that is, "those who defy the law of Allah": "democrats," but also "the crusaders who adore the cross, and believe the Lord of Heaven fathered a child."

[6] This includes 6,788,600 schoolchildren, 3,335,200 11th grade and vocational school (SEGPA) students, 1,498,900 10th grade and technology students, 663,000 students at technical colleges, as well as 214,000 students of the ministries responsible for agriculture and health, and 275 students on apprenticeships or pre-apprenticeships. See "Le Système éducatif," <http://www.education.gouv.fr/pid8/le-systeme-educatif.html> for the current statistics.

of the actors responsible for crisis management, a National Crisis Center was created within the MENESR under the authority of a senior defense and security official, to promote the dissemination of good practice guidelines and feedback. This directive, together with the circulars of November and December 2015, emphasized the importance of meetings at the beginning of school term to inform parents of the security measures in place, and stipulated three exercises to be held during the school year, including an "attack-intrusion" exercise; strengthened security around institutions, and the training of (high-school and college) students in emergency first aid procedures—measures devised to best respond to a global strategy based on the triptych "anticipate, secure, know how to react."[7] In fact, in each of the 101 déepartements, a "general staff" dedicated to the protection of educational institutions has been formed, and the measures mentioned above are being put into effect.[8] The Gendarmerie Nationale, stationed across the whole of the national territory, has committed itself to the effort and has opened three new training centers within the Écoles de Gendarmerie in Rochefort-sur-Mer and Tulle and the École des Officiers de la Gendarmerie Nationale in Melun; from now until September 2018 they will train 500 staff (school principals, Ministry of National Education elementary school inspectors, etc.), compared to 135 in the previous school year. For the "anticipation" element, the government also added a measure calling for training courses designed for managers on issues around crisis management and security, in partnership with the Ecole supérieure de l'Education nationale and the Ecole nationale supérieure de la police.

As for the "secure" element, this was addressed with the allocation of a budget of €50 million in order to accelerate the securitization of the physical premises of schools, colleges, and high schools, and by providing a "practical guide" in partnership with local authorities, which was circulated nationally at the end of March 2017.[9] In our view, we must create "sentinels" who inspire in others a real "vigilance" that is effective and suited to the present state of affairs and to particular circumstances—while maintaining such vigilance for themselves too. As we wrote, "the first duty of a sentinel is to stay alive."[10] One measure is already in effect in some locations, with the visible and deterrent presence of security forces at key moments of the school year (surveillance of the routes of school transport, pickup points, the immediate vicinity

[7] "La sécurité des établissements scolaires, une priorité absolue," <http://www.gouvernement.fr/argumentaire/la-securite-des-etablissements-scolaires-une-priorite-absolue>, January 16, 2017.

[8] According to these directives, all rectors and their teams are to be formed by March 31, 2017.

[9] "It explains security diagnoses and aims to facilitate their implementation by mayors together with the security services of the national police, gendarmerie, and national education personnel (security counselors, national education security services, mobile security teams)." See "Dossier de Presse: Sécurité des écoles, des collèges et des lycées ; procédures de gestion de crise et sécurisation des établissements d'enseignement face à la menace terroriste," March 23, 2017, <http://www.education.gouv.fr/cid114809/securite-des-ecoles-des-colleges-et-des-lycees-nouvelles-mesures-2017.html>.

[10] Raymond H. A. Carter, *Comment se défendre verbalement au quotidien; La parole, arme ultime de la 'communication psychotactique'* (Paris: L'Harmattan, 2016).

of institutions when schoolchildren, students, teachers, and parents assemble, etc.). Other tasks are continuously underway, namely those relating to the securing of the school space[11] together with the updating of the Special Precautionary Plans [Plans Particuliers de Mise en Sûreté, PPMS] and security diagnostics. Note that, since the beginning of the 2016 school year, €13 million (of the €50 million provided) have been fully committed.[12] In 2017, an extra €37 million will be in place to support these projects.

As for "knowing how to react," this is first of all tackled by creating a "handbook" to support the staff of educational institutions.[13] Practical factsheets designed to aid the assimilation of a culture of security[14] and the instinctive reflexes that best serve it have been created in order to provide better support to staff. In addition, joint training in security exercises was trialed with national education staff and heads of groups conducting extracurricular activities; and three déepartements were selected in which to set up joint training, at the national and commune level, of education staff involved with extracurricular activities. These trials sought to "clarify the process and responsibilities of those taking part in the school, at different moments of the child's day" and to "help strengthen the common culture of security for all staff";[15] and finally, "institutions will carry out exercises designed in order to prepare for any potential crisis, in close coordination with local authorities, domestic security forces, and management groups."[16] Some 99 crisis-management exercises had already been organized by prefects in 2016. By the end of the 2016–2017 school year, all eighth-grade schoolchildren (810,000 in all) as well as all high school and

[11] Specifically, in relation to the 131 security measures ("référents sûreté"), and with 2,391 "police-gendarmerie/school security" consultants assisting the heads of institutions to identify which tasks should be prioritized.

[12] 90% of establishments receiving this funding are elementary schools, spread over more than 60 départements.

[13] Five circulars were issued between November 2015 and July 2016, and numerous resources were placed at the disposal of staff.

[14] These factsheets "should allow us to better distinguish the major risks, on one hand, and the 'attack-intrusion' threat on the other, to approach the question of 'attack-intrusion' alarm systems, to clarify the tasks and action levels of measures on the ground, to disseminate instructions for partnership between schools and educational establishments and security forces. The handbook will be published by BOEN on April 13." (See the "Dossier Presse" cited in note 5 above). See in particular "Annexe 1: Mettre à jour le Plan Particulier de Mise en Sûreté PPMS Attentat-intrusion—Guide à destination des directeurs d'école et des chefs d'établissement (Bulletin Officiel n°15 du 13/04/2017)," "Annexe 2 : PPMS « attentat-intrusion »—Fiche pratique à destination des directeurs d'école et des chefs d'établissements: Organiser un exercice « attentat-intrusion »" (Bulletin officiel n°15 du 13/04/2017)," "Annexe 3 : PPMS « attentat-intrusion »—Fiche pratique à destination des directeurs d'école et des chefs d'établissements—l'Alarme « attentat-intrusion » en 8 points (Bulletin officiel n°15 du 13/04/2017)," "Annexe 4: PPMS « attentat-intrusion »—Fiche pratique à destination des directeurs d'école et des chefs d'établissements—Aide au diagnostic de mise en sûreté de l'école ou de l'établissement scolaire (Bulletin officiel n°15 du 13/04/2017)."

[15] See "Dossier Presse" cited in note 5 above.

[16] Ibid.

college students (400,000) will have to have received a course on or an introduction to first aid.

4. Three Levels to Take into Account

As argued in one of our articles,[17] three levels must be taken into account from this perspective of "alertness and openness," moving towards an effective and fruitful vigilance for the good of all, beginning with our youngsters, the future of the nation. These three levels are "the state," throughout the nation; then "the companies" (and "schools") that lie within and between the state and the citizen; and then the citizen himself or herself; each of these levels must come into contact, and must remain in contact, with one another, in a rediscovered "team spirit."

4.1. First Level

The State, throughout the nation, must be "present," with the equipment and human resources to be able to "act" in real "cooperation" and effective "coordination" with all state and national actors, through "genuine collaboration." In particular, the ministries (National Education, Ministry of Security, Ministry of Defense, etc.) to which are attached the civil and military forces of law and order (the National Police, the Gendarmerie, the Army, the Municipal Police, Customs) and the Eemergency services (firefighters, etc.)—and even private security companies where applicable—must work together, in real collaboration and above all with true coordination, in order to effectively succeed in the war against terrorism and other crimes, and must communicate at all times, since communication becomes a priority when faced with terrorism. They must avoid any kind of "isolation" from society, and must make efforts to regenerate a real ongoing contact with citizens at work (companies, etc.) and in their lives (home, school, etc.), following the fine example of the systematic daily work of our "rural guards [*gardes champêtre*]" in their own particular sphere. The directives and measures presented above invite us, at the very minimum, to undertake this kind of "renewal" in "relations" between "the school" and all safety[18] and security[19] actors.

4.2. Second Level

Just as "business" and "businesses," including "schools" in the generic sense we are using the word here—the institutions that constitute the "economic life-

[17] "Le Terrorisme International peut-il être combattu plus efficacement?" (March 29, 2016), by Raymond H. A. Carter, President of the Union des Sociétés d'Education Physique et Préparation Militaire (USEPPM), founded in 1885, officially declared to be in the public interest in 1922.
[18] Relating to any act of wrongdoing (See Carter, "La sûreté des transports").
[19] Relating to any human or technical error (Ibid.).

force" of a country—must keep in contact with one other, they must also keep in contact with the "state organs" discussed above, and with schools and educational establishments. They should be in contact with the state "directly" or "indirectly" (through company "unions"), as well as with the population—that is to say, with the Ccitizen, and with his "offspring," our children. And they must also be in contact and maintain good "internal relations" with their own employees, in order to generate a true spirit of "vigilance," so as to develop within their midst the equipment and human resources to best "secure" (in every sense of the word) their personnel and goods, as well as their activities—to guarantee *intra muros* the requisite "safety" and "security" for their clients, both "direct" (in the place of business) and "indirect" (encountered elsewhere). Businesses must collaborate with the state, and a real and effective "synallagmatism"—if I may be permitted this neologism—should preside over a conjoint action that unites them and permits them to confront criminality in all its forms, beginning with terrorism. Today we must not so much "get used to living with terrorism" as "do everything in our powers to confront and eradicate it within our country."

4.3. Third Level

Here it is a matter of educating *the citizen* as well as the "future citizen" attending school, taking certain actions (information, training, practice, meetings) in order to sensitize them and provide them with the "knowledge" necessary for the adoption of correct attitudes and correct behaviors when faced with any criminal threat (terrorism, organized crime, etc.) whether present, permanent, or even "endemic," through lifesaving "reflexes and gestures"; we shall come back to this below. Our republic can offer an alternative to aimless youths who, out of spite and/or through indoctrination, choose to become radicalized on the basis of false ideas that drive them to commit barbarous acts and even suicide. This alternative may also serve to uncover "lost" potential, thus decreasing the need for surveillance as the subject matures. Is it not our duty to launch a "counter-attack" in order to bring our population together under shared values and with honor, so as to avoid an irrevocable fracture that would play into the hands of these "religious fanatics"?[20]

5. From Theory to Practice

The government directives emphasize the need to organize meetings between all of the "school" and "external" actors presented above. As we like to recall,

[20] During the nineties I observed a scheme of rehabilitation trialed by elite French troops within our army to help wayward young men, who had the choice between three and a half years in prison or twelve months of national service in a disciplinary camp. The results were very encouraging, with a non-recidivism rate of 75%. Some of the subjects who took to military values and military life even made a career of it. As a friend recently suggested to me, doesn't this path of rehabilitation—certainly tough, but fair—deserve to be explored once more, or even adapted to suit the current situation?

"cooperation is good; coordination is better."

5.1. Warning Systems

As indicated in the PPMSs, certain measures must be put in place in respect of warning systems, which constitute "stage one" of reaction. The sounding of an alarm[21] in the presence of danger serves to protect persons (supervisors, students, etc.) from danger and to prompt an "appropriate reaction." In certain circumstances, depending on the site, this can be done "silently" so as to reduce as far as possible any panic and anxiety as events unfold. In addition, the use of "beepers,"[22] designed to warn someone at a distance when the person *in situ* (agent, teacher, etc.) sounds the alarm, would allow law enforcement to be alerted discreetly and effectively, while leading endangered students toward a "protected" place designated in advance and maintained for such a purpose; thus allowing law enforcement to intervene wisely, rapidly, and effectively, fully informed as to the location and cause. "To protect is good, to defend is better!"

5.2. Securitization/Protection Systems

Whatever scenario is used for the "attack-intrusion" exercise,[23] "escape" or "lock in," order and rigor of movement must be uppermost, so as to ensure awareness of the "more haste, less speed" principle and guarantee an "effective system."[24] The "escape" option must be optimally "secured" in order to avoid making students an easy prey for terrorist gunmen, and should be adapted appropriately to the site or sites in question. If the "lock in" scenario is used, we strongly recommend the construction of one or several rooms that can be sealed effectively with equipment capable of blocking all fire coming from without. The reliability of such equipment should permit the implementation of highly effective systems able to foil terrorist attacks and bombings against persons and property, whether private or public. Within schools and educational institutions, an "Assessment and Audit of Security and Safety"[25] will allow the identification of strong and weak points of the institution in

[21] A specific system, audio alarm, foghorn, siren, etc. which would be chosen by the head of the educational institution.

[22] It is not a self-evident move to call a number ("911") when one is directly under the pressure of a "present, wrongful, and real" threat, and the facts prove it, sometimes even with men who have been "trained" for a "necessary, simultaneous, and proportionate" defense.

[23] Systematically divided into three phases: 1. Preparation of the exercise; 2. Sensitization; 3. Realization of the exercise, before an evaluation/RETEX by the participants (from the school) and/or external observers (law enforcement, municipality, etc.)

[24] The students cannot be left unsupervised, and in particular cannot be allowed to run at will randomly, since this would place them in grave danger when faced with fanatical gunmen.

[25] Of the institution, the environment, the external surroundings, fence, access points and their control, the perimeter space between the access points and/or the buildings, the securing of access points and/or "panic rooms," etc.

question. In order to better guard against any attack, systems can be installed within and outside the institution.[26]

5.2.1. Within the Institution

Within the institution, the creation of one or more secure rooms of the "panic room" type in one or more suitable places, modified to match the general appearance of the institution, should make it possible for students, teachers, and staff of the institution in order to take shelter until the arrival of the competent law enforcement and special units. A specific material made to strengthen the security of these "security rooms," which can stop any bullet up to and including a Kalashnikov bullet (up to 2,500 Joules) would be the ideal for this kind of room, since one or many "classes" of weapons currently in use can be dealt with in this way. These requirements are met by "SQUAMA," produced by Rigomer Engineering, which can stop bullets moving with a force of up to 5,300 Joules[27]; it seems to us among the most effective and easily adaptable materials with which to create this type of "panic room," as demonstrated by the results of tests carried out at a distance of 5m from the aforementioned "SQUAMA." The technologies and research projects of Rigomer Engineering in France seem to us particularly interesting and "ahead of the game" in confronting the new terrorist threats and actions more effectively, particularly in terms of prevention and intervention, and in their contribution to a better fight against modern terrorism. This ballistic protection allows the distribution of the force (pressure) of any projectile that strikes the aggregates integrated into the zone of assembly, which then in turn strikes aluminum honeycombs, developed by Renaud Rigomer and Olivier Poisson of the company AFL Foessel, directed by M. Patrick Poisson for this particular field of application, across a 25 times larger zone, transmitting the movement (imperceptible to the naked eye and at real speed) to the panels that make up the wall, which can be designed and arranged according to

---

[26] Video surveillance systems can also be installed for optimal surveillance of sites by state, municipal, or private services, allowing observation of events at the moment of the attack and in any legal process that follows.

[27] Based on the principles of tribology (the study of surfaces in friction) and "controlled displacement," the Rigomer Engineering technology, to explain it as simply as possible, turns "the energy of the aggressor" against itself, redirecting it into a harmless zone and absorbing the greater part of its force by means of honeycomb aluminum cartridges made by the company AFT, which are fusible elements. Inspired by the study of martial arts techniques, and in particular Aikido, this technology allows one to more effectively "steer" aggression so as to control it and "turn it back on the adversary proportionately." The SQUAMA stops many 7.62×39 (Kalashnikov) bullets, steel core bullets which reach a force of 2,300 joules, and shots of large hunting caliber such as the 300 Win and the 9.3×62 all steel alloy bullet which reach a force of between 5,100 and 5,300 joules at a distance of ten meters from the protective surface, as we have ourselves been able to verify. Rigomer Engineering SAS, Combreux, France—contact@rigomer.com, <http://rigomer.com>.

operational need. Rigomer Engineering also carries out research on other products,[28] in particular for protection against detonations.[29]

5.2.2. Outside in the surrounding area

Here either "fixed" or "mobile" systems can be deployed.

5.2.2.1. "Fixed systems"

As well as a possible video surveillance system, it is possible to station at the entrance and at "other weak points" an "anti-intrusion" system against a "vehicle battering ram" likely to transport criminals or explosives; this is the "ANTARIES," a freestanding "anti-passage obstacle" that is discrete, reusable, and economical, developed for the securing of specific zones (frontages, retaining walls, etc.) of an establishment (store, school, etc.). Having stopped a vehicle (vehicle-ram, etc.), the replacement of its (consumable) aluminum "cartridge" will restore its capacities in full. It can be customized in such a way as to blend in aesthetically with the surrounding decor without its presence being suspected. It can also be used, for safety and security purposes, by law enforcement (Gendarmerie, Police, Customs, Municipal Police, etc.) and their special units (SWAT teams, etc.) as well as by private companies for use in private properties they are responsible for safeguarding.[30]

5.2.2.2. "Mobile" systems

Here it is once again a question of providing local law enforcement (Municipal

---

[28] Individual protective gilets and t-shirts based on the same technology as SQUAMA, protective shields, electric tonfa batons, anti-intrusion doors, quite "revolutionary" "lockers" for explosion containment or the adding of protection to an already-existing wall, and—of the greatest interest to us in the current context—"anti-explosion partitions" for all manner of access points into public sites with heavy footfall (airports, stations, exhibition fairs, etc.), which are now viable, and can be made with the same kind of functionality—namely, "to absorb the blast by redirecting its energy in non-lethal directions."

[29] These products need to achieve the displacement of molecules of oxygen (in blast effects) at speeds ranging from 350m/second to 750m/second for "homemade" explosives, which are our concern here; but the same technique can handle all types of explosives in use today. According to the ballistics research carried out by and still underway at Rigomer Engineering, a very satisfactory mechanical behavior and aptitude at speeds of 950 and 1,115m/second (which still leaves a large margin with this technology) have been observed; this provided the motive for a "meeting" with our fundamental French-German research (ISL), where the staff and research director confirmed the capacity of Rigomer Engineering to manage explosive blasts through absorption and redirection of the blast, highlighting that the aforementioned company of Renaud Rigomer was fifteen years ahead of the state of the art in current research.

[30] The ANTARIES is robust, 70 kg in weight, made of steel, and allows a 2-ton vehicle traveling at 64 km/h to be stopped. It is fixed to the ground, or ideally onto a 450-kg steel plate, which increases the absorption of kinetic energy upon impact.

Police, Gendarmerie, and National Police) with equipment that is transportable and can be placed according to the layout of the site (on roads, streets, etc.) and the "circumstances" (recess time, entrance and exit, etc.) in order to block, if need be, roads and other access points while permitting the interception of vehicles. The system in question is a "RATEL," a mobile vehicles interceptor which, like the ANTARIES, is freestanding and reusable, thanks to the same aluminum cartridges. It was developed by Intervention Groups, particularly in Special Forces units.[31] Whatever happens, before and during or after the intervention of law enforcement, the imperative order to "touch no object," whether suspect or not, left behind by the assailants, is an indispensable basic rule which must be communicated to both staff and students of the institution under attack, as stated in the "information/training." The alert will be lifted by law enforcement.

6. Information and Training

The adoption of a "precautionary mindset" and the development of "correct reactions" takes place through "theoretical information and training" and "practical training" that is realistic and well-adapted to its audience, rendered simple and effective so as to strike the minds of "students," whatever their age may be, in the most natural way.

6.1. Theoretical Information/Training

"Theoretical information/training" of a "participative" nature must aim to sensitize students and staff, realistically but without paranoia, and should involve a "dialogue" on the different "themes" linked to the present context and current affairs, moving toward a "pragmatic relationship," through questions and answers, to yield "the correct responses" in the case of attack or intrusion. Personally, we often pose the same question: what would we do in our own home, for our family and ourselves? This training should be based on information about what terrorism is and what "terrorists" are; and delivered in such a way as to heighten the "vigilance" of one and all. Subsequently, as well as a better understanding of their "school," which becomes a place of "survival,"[32] a certain number of "issues" must also be brought forward in order to know the adversary better, to adapt, and to learn how to improvise on "non-improvised" bases. The more one is "trained," the more one practices, the less "anxiogenic" a situation will be. Fear does not deliver us from danger, so we

---

[31] The RATEL is a 48-kg freestanding, easily transportable "mobile vehicles interceptor" equipped with an economical and replaceable aluminum cartridge. With dimensions of 941 × 52w × 45h cm, it allows the interception of a 2-ton vehicle at a speed of 64 km/h. Simple to set up, easy to maintain, using a patented process for energy dissipation through the translation of mass based on the principles of tribology, the RATEL can immobilize any vehicle that tries to force its way past, and is suitable for all types of terrain.

[32] Carter, "Guide pratique de survie en zone urbaine et campagne."

should try instead to identify it (terrorist attack, etc.) so as to better cope with and confront it.

6.2. "Practical" Training

"Practical" training via good knowledge of the site (the school) and its actors and occupants (teachers, staff, etc.) so as to adopt adequate "movements" within the premises, averting any "panic" in reaction to an attack and minimizing "disorder," and to regroup in one or several "secured" places, through "practical exercises" realized in "real-world" conditions. With younger children, these movements could be studied in the form of a "game." The primary objective here is to elicit an appropriate reaction/action, with a minimum of panic, so as to "turn back the time" of the aggressor to advance that of the "savior"—in this case the agents of law enforcement. If, as the apostle Paul says, "I have the right to do anything, but not everything is beneficial," let us avoid the "non-beneficial." We must learn to be conscious of the danger in order to better control it.

In "elementary schools," promote the "ludic" over the "tragic." The game "king of silence" where everyone must stay quiet, and the first to speak is out, may be useful here—why not! The fact is that we must "act" in order to "react" better! "Self-defense" must justify "pre-emptive action"; for "learning to defend myself" does not mean "I love to fight"—quite the contrary! "To fight is to move," and one can "learn to fight" other than with one's fists—with language, with "Verbal Defense," for example;[33] one can learn to move within and get to know a "habitat," to "make friends" with it so that it does not become a "maze" when the hour of "survival" comes. The training should allow children to make their "school" a "special," "friendly," "safe" place within which students take on their share of responsibility and initiative, becoming conscious of dangers and "circumscribing" them in space (in the playground, in the stairway, in the building, etc.) and in time (upon entering, during the day and particularly at recess, on exiting). They should be able to create a "simulation exercise": "To the shelters"!

The "trinomial" above (information/training/practice) is a must for anyone who wishes to confront a situation of "stress"[34] under optimal conditions. Exercises, from the "playful" to the "serious" depending on the age of the "students," and always rooted in reality, must be brought together with other skills such as "stress management" in order to decrease fear and anxiety, "cardiac coherence," "verbal defense," and others familiar to us, all of them constituting interesting means and responses for learning to "manage oneself" when faced with an urgent situation. In this way, discipline and cohesion are strengthened and become sure allies, indispensable "partners," and "comrades" that we must get to know and frequent.

[33] Carter, *Comment se défendre verbalement au quotidien.*
[34] Raymond H.A. Carter and Yves Le Mee, *Stress et Défense Personnelle, ou Bien s'en sortir en cas d'agression* (Paris: Chiron, 2006).

7. Problems and Proposals

The elements mentioned above deserve to be taken into consideration, given the "practical" side that they can bring into the daily life of Man, whatever his age may be. Information and training must promote "personal preparedness" (whether professional or not) when faced with terrorist risks and threats, permitting the latter to be better anticipated, either upstream of the "problem," during it, or after it.

"Without making matters worse," it is a matter of informing students and staff about the terrorist threats and risks that surround their everyday life, of awakening their vigilance through specific information and training tailored for "pre-emption" and "self-defense." They should be informed about the nature of reactions: how to react and act when faced with an attack or a terrorist bombing, particularly on the basis of the four points I have developed for "survival," namely (1) Hide/lie down, (2) Drink, (3) Eat, and (4) Move[35] as well as elements of first aid and the development of contact with "the Other," the civil and military authorities. It can also involve role-playing based on "feedback" that informs us about the reality of conflict situations of all types that might be encountered on the ground, in everyday life, and in all sorts of circumstances. Alongside this can go as specific specialized training, such as "verbal defense," which teaches methods of intervention when faced with verbal aggression, so as to avoid or to maximally "defer" all physical aggression, through techniques that can be adapted depending on the circumstances, drawing on psychotactical communication, theories of motivation, stress management, therapies, professional intervention, the principle of disinterest, and self-defense.[36] "Stress management" with role-playing is a type of training during which stress and aggression are defined, along with the reactions one should have to them depending on the circumstances and places where the "problem" arises,[37] in order to best regulate them. Urban and rural "survival" techniques equip the individual to face any "social circumstance," even in the most difficult moments.[38] "Self-defense of oneself and others" enables one to face aggression against oneself and/or others with suitable and effective techniques of personal defense, guided by the experience of instructors, and many works of the author of the present document.[39]

---

[35] Raymond H. A. Carter, *Guide pratique de survie en zone urbaine et campagne* (Paris: L'Harmattan, 2014).

[36] Carter, *Comment se défendre verbalement au quotidien.*

[37] Carter and Le Mee, *Stress et Défense Personnelle.*

[38] Carter, *Guide pratique de survie en zone urbaine et campagne.*

[39] In particular Raymond H.A. Carter and Kim Oriol, Techniques de Combat au corps-à-corps, vols 1, 2, and 3 (Paris: Chiron, 1991); Raymond H. A. Carter, Technique de combat au couteau—Knife Fighting techniques (Paris: Chiron, 1996); Raymond H.A. Carter and Pascal Boyard, La Boxe Thaïlandaise et le Kick-Boxing (Paris: Chiron, 1997); Raymond H.A. Carter, Combat et Défense Aquatiques (Paris: Chiron, 2007); Raphaël and Olivier Saint-Vincent, Le Close Combat: Techniques et entraînements (Paris: Chiron, 2006), vols 1, 2 et 3. This training, along with others incorporated into "safety" and "security," are provided by the company Cormoran-Group SAS, <http://www.cormorangroup.fr>.

8. Conclusion

Terrorism today is increasingly disfiguring our society and others, which, like ours, continue to try and maintain confidence in Man, whatever may be the cost, despite his inconstancy, his fickle and unstable side, and the increasingly evident egotism that lies within him.

And even though "there is no such thing as absolute security," there is nothing to prevent us from coming closer to it and keeping "insecurity" contained in space and time, protecting our integrity and that of our fellow citizens. In a society where liberty does not always imply taking account of "the Other," and where "rights" increasingly supplant "duty," it is important to arm oneself and to be on guard sufficiently on a personal level so as to be able to face a daily life rendered increasingly difficult by those who respect neither the social framework that accommodates them, nor the rights and duties of Man, which must remain in balance for the happiness and salvation of all. Each must know himself in order to better know and recognize the Other. Only in this way will we be recognized in turn. Hence the necessity of understanding and improving our knowledge of social phenomena, certainly; but also that of knowing how to reassess things and being prepared to do so when necessary, for his happiness and that of his neighbor, as well as that of our "descendants." A return to the social values of our societies is necessary. We owe homage to other police and gendarmes, including our comrades in the GIGN, for what they do every day, often faced with the greatest indifference from those who owe them their "security" and "peace."

So yes, we believe that terrorism can be combatted more effectively, on condition that we are given the means, and that we know how to assess it. As we have written: "There is no such thing as a strong man, there are only well-trained men."

April 30, 2017
Raymond H.A. Carter

Research Notes:

Building an Efficient Data Vault for a Corrections Environment Using SCRUM and AGILE Techniques for Operational Business Intelligence

Gary Harmon

Chapter 1: Data Vault for Big Human Data

The Data Vault methodology allows for best practices from a variety of different components that allow for unparalleled flexibility. The problem in Big Data, as explained by the Corrections Technology Association in its presentation "Big Data and Corrections: What's the Big Issue?", is that Corrections Data is growing at an astounding rate due to the fact that nearly 1 in 33 adults in the United States is under correctional control and that "Human" data in a correctional system is different. "Human Information is made up of ideas, is diverse, and has context. Ideas do not exactly match like data do; they have distance. Human Information is not static; it is dynamic and lives everywhere. Legacy techniques have all fallen short" (Corrections Technology Association 2013). They also cite that with the mixture of data coming in from so many different sources, it creates an increased risk. This increased risk can be uniquely put to a halt by using a Data Vault. The Data Vault will allow for multiple types of data to be accounted for while providing data integrity to key business facts.

Quantity and Quality in the State Correctional System

The Criminal Justice Organizations are beginning to create more advanced data management systems to collect, store, and process large amounts of data. This enables correctional organizations the ability to lower the overall risk associated within a corrections environment by using data to make smart and analytical decisions. It further facilitates advanced management of correctional facilities by giving organizations a data-centered strategic policy. However, the sheer volume of data inside many correctional databases often poses complexity and quality concerns. The success of any major data system depends on the quality of the data that is stored in it. This quality control can be managed by the Data Vault in a specific way that allows for key business facts to remain intact while allowing for scalability based on the environment.

When looking at State Correctional Systems, 3 states have more than 100,000 inmates in custody, 15 states have 20,000-–50,000 inmates in custody, and all other State Correctional Systems have less than 20,000 inmates per state with a combined total of only 289,475 inmates (Carson 2015). This would suggest that California, Florida, and Texas, whose inmates in custody combine to an amount higher than that of 34 states combined, would have far more complex data quality issues than other states based only on the amount of information per inmate. However, when using a Data Vault system, the complexity of the data may increase as the size increases, but the integrity and quality of the most important data will not change. The unique connection between the Inmate ID in corrections management and the architecture of the Data Vault for business intelligence allows the integrity of the Inmate ID to pass over to the Data Vault and create a unique identification tool for quality control.

Chapter 2: Correctional Environments and Their Operational Connections to Data Vaults

In order to explain the importance of the Data Vault system for a correctional environment, it is imperative that one first understands the correctional environment. The correctional environment is filled with ranging skill sets, from those with little to no technical knowledge (who often serve on operational fronts), to those with novice to medium technical skill levels who serve as support staff to operational staff. There is often a small number of people who have a technical skill set above medium. This range of skill sets is important to this application because it will not only show the value of the Data Vault in this particular industry, but will show the Data Vaults' qualities because of the way this particular industry operates.

The correctional environment revolves around two key business facts:. (1) The inmate resides in housing provided by the Government, whether it be privately monitored or not, the housing is still provided by the Government. (2) The inmate has certain physical characteristics that will not change outside of the normal scope of human progression. An inmate will age just like any other person. An inmate will have specific physiological characteristics such as eye color, hair color, weight, height, race, gender, and so on.

Now, with those two key business facts an inmate is also given a unique identifier known as a unique identification number or Inmate ID that is specific to only that inmate and no one else. This Inmate ID works as a unique identifier. The primary data source in a Corrections Data Management System or (CMS) is entered by the end user when the inmate arrives at the diagnostic intake center. At this point, the inmate's data becomes active and the inmate is given an Inmate ID. This does not happen if the inmate has been in prison before. All inmates entering diagnostic are checked by an Iris Biometric Scanner to ensure connection to correct Inmate ID. The secondary data source in a CMS is entered by users at the local facility, regional headquarters, or at the main headquarters' locations. This unique identifier serves an important purpose when presenting the idea of using a Data Vault in a correctional environment. It allows the vault to be built around one centralized unchanging ID that will hold the key to data integrity. This ID is specific to one inmate and one inmate only, which allows the Data Vault to be built around that fact. It also allows the Data Vault to serve a Small Enterprise System with only 100–200 total inmates, while also being able to serve a Large Enterprise System with as many as 150,000 inmates. The reason for this is that the Data Integrity is based upon the industry standard of one unique identifier for one inmate. This one-to-one connection means that a system with 150,000 inmates will have 150,000 unique identifiers active at any given time while a system with 250 inmates will have 250 unique identifiers active at any given time. In addition to the data integrity in current time that is forced into the Data Vault by the operational aspects of the correctional industry's Inmate ID as a unique identifier the data integrity of the historical data is also protected. The correctional industry's one inmate ID to one inmate operational security in turn protects historical data because Inmate 1 can never be Inmate 6 Million. These inmates could have the same name, same tattoos, same birthdates, and have every other physiological and psychological connection, but would still be able to be uniquely identified based on the fact that Inmate 1's unique identifier and Inmate 6 Millions' can and never will be the same.

According to Dan Linstedt the "Data Vault represents a system of business intelligence" (Linstedt and Olschimke 2015, p. 11). The correctional industry feeds off of business intelligence making it a prime location for a Data Vault system. The Data Vault system allows for a correctional environment to house the business intelligence it needs and be able to quantify that information based on the industry's unique identification standards of the Inmate ID. The Data Vault system also presents another a unique feature that is in perfect correlation with a correctional environment's ecosystem and its connection to politics.

In R.A. Mcgee's *Prisons and Politics*, published by the National Criminal Justice Reference Service, the author makes a clear connection between state politics and correctional policy roles and legislation. "The State executive branch is presented as the initiator of broad correctional policy. The roles of the Governor are described as political, symbolic and ceremonial, policymaking, administrative, coordinating, and legislative. The performances of the various Governors under which the author has served as a correctional administrator are portrayed. The discussion of the legislative branch's influence on corrections gives particular attention to the situation in California (NCJRS n.d.).". Even though Mr. Mcgee's information looked at the pre-1980 politics, the information still holds true based on the organizational charts of many state governments in reference to corrections where the head of the department is directly appointed by the governor of the state. "The Michigan Department of Corrections is one of the principal state departments. Final responsibility for operation of the department rests with the Governor who appoints the Director, with the advice and consent of the state Senate. The Director serves at the pleasure of the Governor (Corrections Organizational Structure n.d.)". In order to fully understand a correctional environment, it is imperative that the changing political structure be acknowledged not as a mere side note in the ecosystem but as one of its most pivotal and structural measures.

The Need for Data Vaults in Correctional Systems

For business processes the Data Vault, as a data integration architecture, has robust standards and definitional methods which unite information in order to make sense of it. However, one of the most robust systems ever created for the State of California did not use Data Vault Architecture, according to Bill Inmon's "The Data Vault is the Optimal Choice for Modeling the EDW in the DW 2.0 framework" (Inmon, Strauss, and Neushloss 2008). The Data Vault is a modeling technique that is able to accommodate three important aspects of Big Data in corrections: integrity of key inmate identification data; addition and tracking of new data; and the ability to separate historical data from current data. Now just because it attacks these three main points does not mean that it does not also increase other important business facts in corrections such as speed, efficiency, and the ability to make sense of data. The Data Vault approach for a correctionals environment will allow for simplification in the data entry process by allowing for segregation of data aspects. End users will be able to use one satellite to identify the data to be entered preventing it from being entered incorrectly based on pre-set conventions. Using the Data Vault system architecture a correctional system will be able to allow non-technical users to focus their efforts on efficient and agile operational problem solving using actionable business intelligence instead of waiting on a technical user to produce, decipher, and deliver the business intelligence needed. This happens by first allowing new data sources to be added as they become available without having to disrupt the original data schema. Second, the unique structure of the operational system of corrections and the Inmate ID allows for business intelligence software to be comfortably placed on top of the Data Vault with a unique identifier that allows for multiple applications. The ability to change what business intelligence the operational staff see and are able to decipher without the aid of anything else is an integral part of the equation. As noted before, criminal justice reform may change based on the political structure of the state or nation and the need for additional data points becomes imperative to tracking progress of new reforms and objectives that are put into place. Those new reforms and objectives are able to then be transferred by using Data Vault 2.0 technology to catapult the business intelligence software into the arms of the operational staff in a visually acceptable way that will allow them to be operationally significant.

Chapter 3: SCRUM and Agile Best Practices for Corrections

One of the biggest aspects of SCRUM is helping the team to eliminate anything that is slowing them down. In order to account for the waste of data in corrections, a look into the context of Big Data and the 3V structure is warranted first.

The context of Big Data in corrections is described best by looking at the 3V structure that is present in the data: volume, velocity, and variety. Volume can be explained by the sheer volume of inmates in the United States, therefore creating the sheer volume of data inside a correctional database. The variety of information needed about these individuals to be able to house them safely and securely can range from gang ties to vegan diets. Last, the velocity or speed needed to keep end users equipped with the ever-changing amount of data that exists from the various complexities that exist inside of a correctional ecosystem.

The CMMI Maturity level 5 focuses on continually improving process performance through both incremental and innovative technological improvements (Team 2006). The key words in this definition in relation to correctional environments are incremental and innovative. Correctional environments use the logic of changing a process in a slow and methodical way as not to disturb the current environment too much at one time. They also have to look at innovative ways to deal with problems that other organizations would not have to deal with in relation to technology improvements. A quick example will explain how this works: In a normal business environment a process can be implemented using negative or positive reinforcement. In a correctional environment the lack of a positive or negative repercussion means that efforts that do not depend on positive or negative repercussion must sometimes be developed. In a normal business environment an employee wants to keep his or her job, wants to avoid being incarcerated, and wants to go home after work. In a correctional environment these three outlooks are null and void. This means that the physical security of data and the non-physical security of data have to be changed to fit the environment. Data Vault 2.0 technology will be used to allow for optimization by evaluating quantitative process-improvement objectives, monitoring continually changing business objectives, and keeping the data secure.

SCRUM allows the Data Vault structure to take the volume and variety of the data down to allow for better velocity. This is done in the same way operational variety and volume in a correctional environment is separated. In a typical correctional environment there is a warden who oversees a prison. That warden is only responsible for inmates under his jurisdiction at his/her prison. The warden is not concerned with an operational sense with inmates at another prison except in rare cases where situations from the enterprise system may bleed from one prison to another. The variety of inmates and the volume of inmates have been cut down so that a warden is able to safely and effectively manage a prison at an acceptable velocity. If that is the operational standard, why would the warden need data from the other prisons to operate his prison at an optimal velocity? The Data Vault structure allows the data to be separated in a way that allows for the variety of the data to be reduced, the volume of the data to be reduced without affecting the operational aspects but by actually allowing for scalability which in turn will improve them by using SCRUM-based priority structures. Instead of taking the traditional approach to all data, it is important that the warden is able to look at what data is most important to his/her facility and focus on that information. This approach allows for the different missions of different prisons to be scaled into the actual Data Vault structure. In the current correctional climate, there exist three main prison missions in most correctional systems that effect the operational structure of the prison: re-entry into society, medium to low security, and high security. The Data Vault structure allows for these three missions to operate off of separate hubs and satellites based on the SCRUM-based main priority of the prison. A re-entry prison does not need information about death row and a high-security prison does not need information about work release assignments because those items do not exist operationally at those facilities. If the operational aspect is not there it only makes sense that data for the operational aspect that is not needed also be absent and not part of any prioritization.

Data Entry and Staging

Data entry will occur at two levels in the Correctional Database Systems Management Solution. The first will occur upon first admittance to the prison system via iris biometric admittance verification at diagnostic intake. This biometric classification to one inmate ID insures the data integrity of his Inmate ID, and will be the first point of record. The information entered at this point will be classified into hub H_Admission noting that the inmate has been admitted and whether or not it is the inmate's first trip to prison. Then information will be entered into the hub H_Inmate_Main. The second level of data entry will occur when a facility enters information about an inmate. Information obtained at this point will be information about an inmate's whereabouts, actions that an inmate commits, programming, counseling, meals, medical, and so on. The third level of data entry will occur at the location of the main headquarters. Information entered by the headquarters' location will be specific to incarceration and will be entered into the hub H_Incarceration.

The staging area will be used to hold raw data and then move it into the data warehouse. Information that will go into the operational Data Vault includes information concerning operational aspects of the inmate while under control of a correctional system. Information will then be declassified and passed into a non-operational Data Vault. This will allow information deemed operational to be used for research purposes without interrupting the operational aspects of the correctional system's main Business Vault.

Operational Business Intelligence

One of the secondary objectives of creating a prototype for a correctional environment that was based on a Data Vault architecture was to have operationally functional business intelligence. The reason the business intelligence needed to be visually optimized was to properly serve the operational use case. The operational use case requires a user to be able to point and click their way to the desired information. In order for this to happen the business intelligence has to look and feel a way that the user is able to easily identify with for operational use. Now, while this might not be technically important to the data integrity or other technical aspects of the Data Vault and business intelligence, it plays a significant role in the operational use case that the business intelligence will play.

The business intelligence software is positioned on top of the Data Vault structure in a way that allows the user to be able to access information in an operational environment for an operational purpose. The end user does not have to figure out which way to count the information that is provided to them. The end user does not have to figure out which sets of data are operationally important that information is provided to them in a dashboard structure that is pre-approved during the design phase. The business intelligence instead of creating a roadblock for a non-technical end user creates a platform for actual business intelligence. The next example will explain how this process would work.

Due to the recent examinations of policy all members of street gangs who have been incarcerated for violent offenses must attend counseling at least 3 days a week.

Figure 3.1. Database diagram of Information used for business intelligence

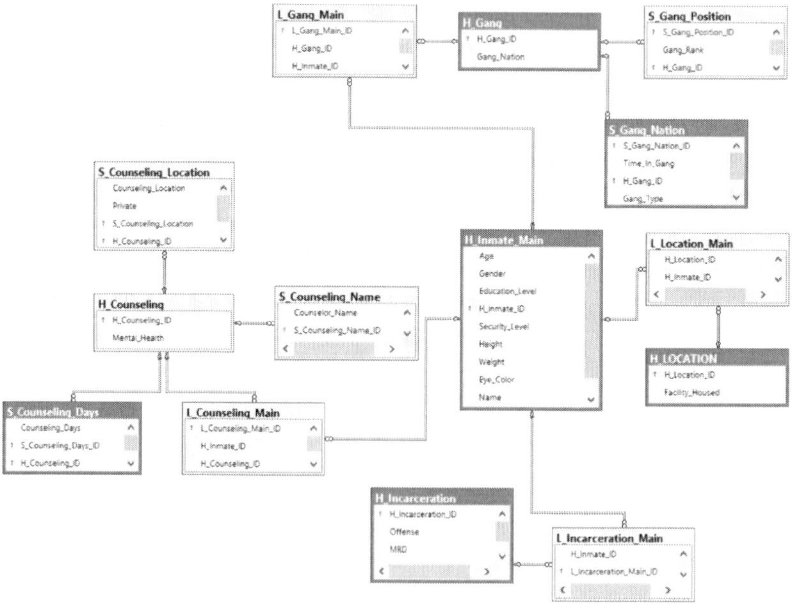

The dashboard for the end user has already been set up to only identify the Users Facility G4, identify known gang members, identify counseling days as either TH for those needing 2 days a week, or MWF for those needing 3 days a week.

The end user is able to use the pre-designed dashboard to identify that they have four members of a street gang.

Figure 3.2.

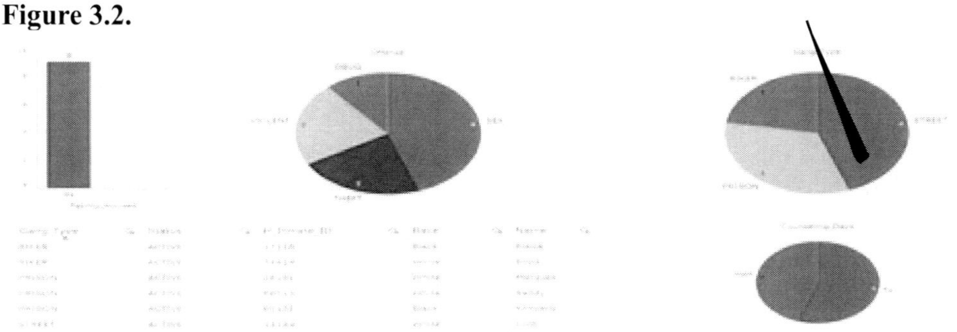

Figure 3.3. They are then able to identify that one has a violent history.

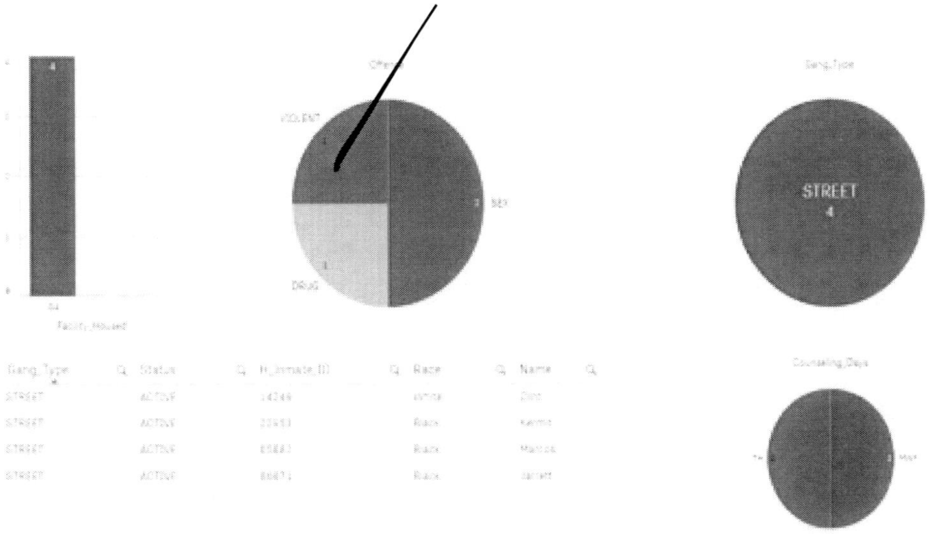

Now from the business intelligence software the end user with only two mouse clicks the has identified that the operational decision needs to be made to have Inmate Marcos's schedule changed from TH to MWF.

Figure 3.4.

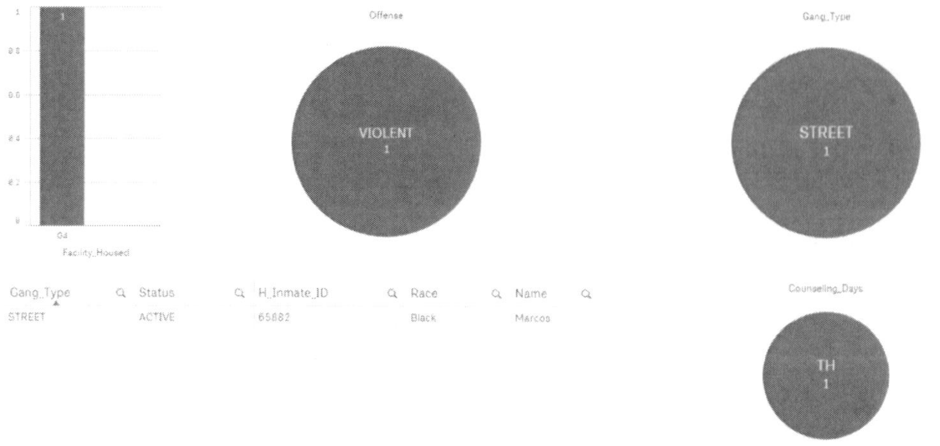

Figure 3.5. SQL of business intelligence for Figure 3.4.

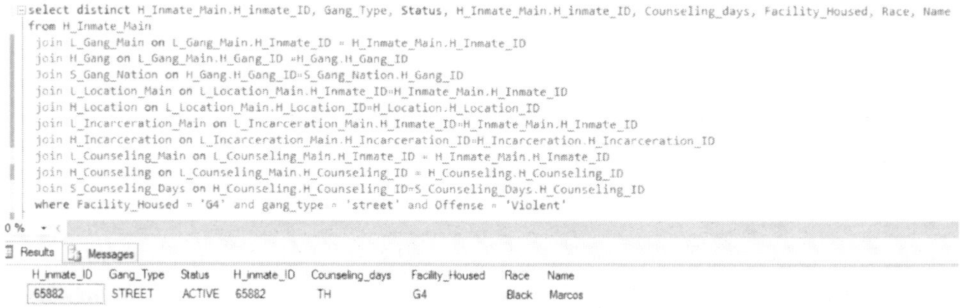

```
select distinct H_Inmate_Main.H_inmate_ID, Gang_Type, Status, H_Inmate_Main.H_inmate_ID, Counseling_days, Facility_Housed, Race, Name
from H_Inmate_Main
 join L_Gang_Main on L_Gang_Main.H_Inmate_ID = H_Inmate_Main.H_Inmate_ID
 join H_Gang on L_Gang_Main.H_Gang_ID =H_Gang.H_Gang_ID
 Join S_Gang_Nation on H_Gang.H_Gang_ID=S_Gang_Nation.H_Gang_ID
 join L_Location_Main on L_Location_Main.H_Inmate_ID=H_Inmate_Main.H_Inmate_ID
 join H_Location on L_Location_Main.H_Location_ID=H_Location.H_Location_ID
 join L_Incarceration_Main on L_Incarceration_Main.H_Inmate_ID=H_Inmate_Main.H_Inmate_ID
 join H_Incarceration on L_Incarceration_Main.H_Incarceration_ID=H_Incarceration.H_Incarceration_ID
 join L_Counseling_Main on L_Counseling_Main.H_Inmate_ID = H_Inmate_Main.H_Inmate_ID
 join H_Counseling on L_Counseling_Main.H_Counseling_ID = H_Counseling.H_Counseling_ID
 Join S_Counseling_Days on H_Counseling.H_Counseling_ID=S_Counseling_Days.H_Counseling_ID
 where Facility_Housed = 'G4' and gang_type = 'street' and Offense = 'Violent'
```

Results | Messages

H_inmate_ID	Gang_Type	Status	H_inmate_ID	Counseling_days	Facility_Housed	Race	Name
65882	STREET	ACTIVE	65882	TH	G4	Black	Marcos

The previous example showed how the information could be used operationally at the local level but the same business model could be used for an enterprise-wide application. In addition, if the information is needed to be changed the same business intelligence dashboard can serve a dual purpose as long as the information resides in one of the predefined tables. Instead of looking at local violent offenders the business question has been changed to those who have committed sex-related offenses.

Due to the recent examinations of policy all members of street gangs who have been incarcerated for sex offenses must attend counseling at least 3 days a week.

Figure 3.6. Fourteen street gang members across all facilities.

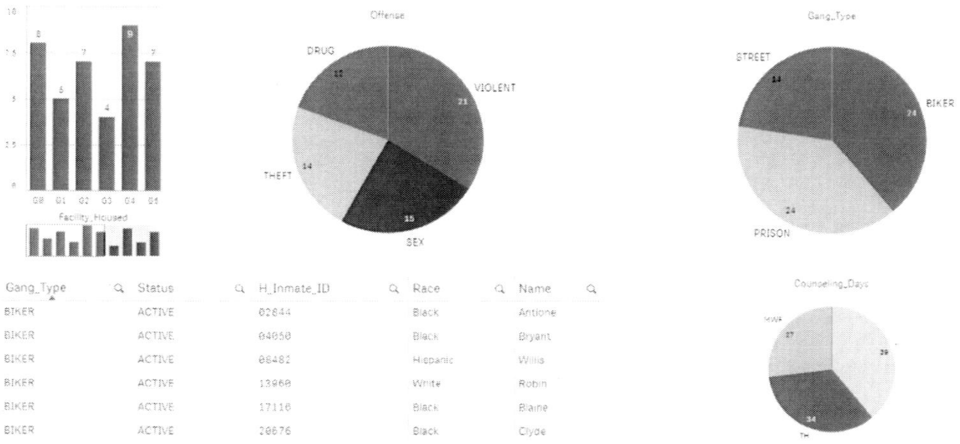

Figure 3.7. Three are incarcerated for sex offenses.

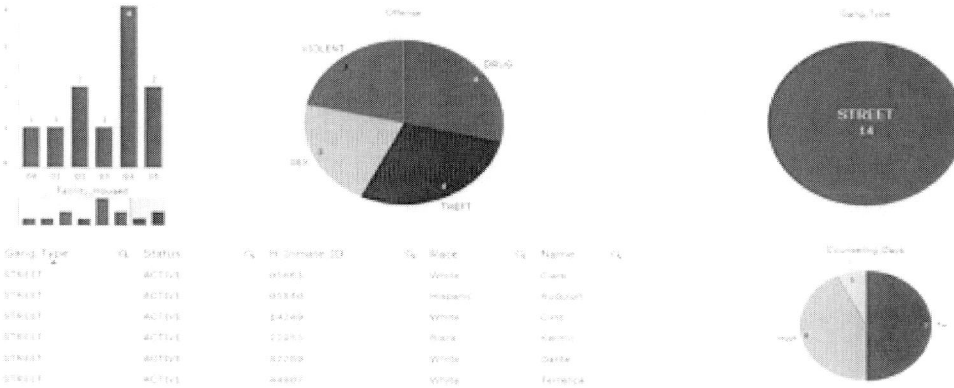

Figure 3.8. One does not have a 3-day counseling schedule.

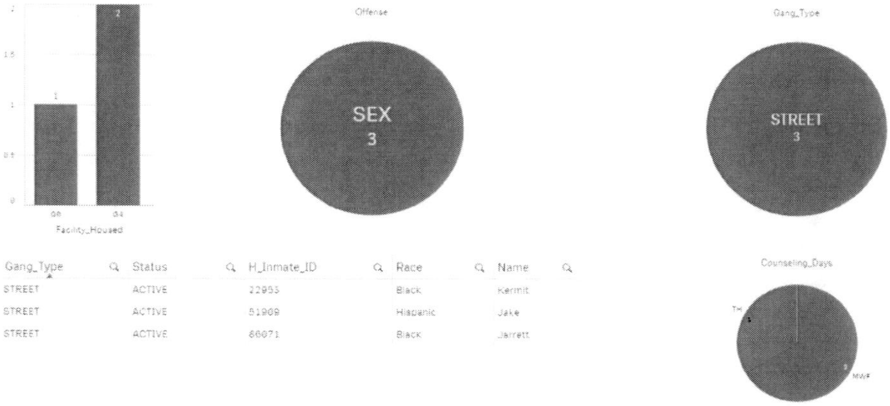

Now from the business intelligence gained the operational decision that a call needs to be made to Facility G0 to inform them that Inmate Jake needs to have a counseling schedule changed can occur.

Figure 3.9.

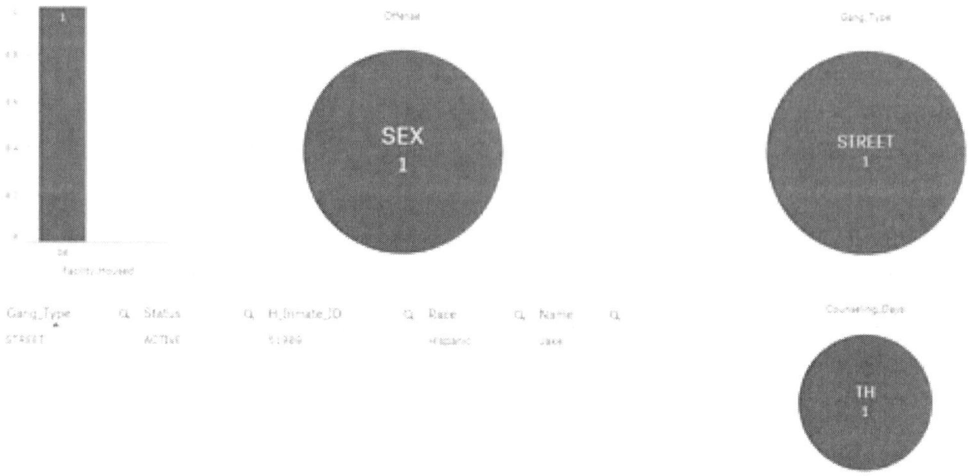

Figure 3.10. SQL of business intelligence for Figure 3.9.

```sql
select distinct H_Inmate_Main.H_inmate_ID, Gang_Type, Status, H_Inmate_Main.H_inmate_ID, Counseling_days, Facility_Housed, Race, Name
from H_Inmate_Main
 join L_Gang_Main on L_Gang_Main.H_Inmate_ID = H_Inmate_Main.H_Inmate_ID
 join H_Gang on L_Gang_Main.H_Gang_ID =H_Gang.H_Gang_ID
 Join S_Gang_Nation on H_Gang.H_Gang_ID=S_Gang_Nation.H_Gang_ID
 join L_Location_Main on L_Location_Main.H_Inmate_ID=H_Inmate_Main.H_Inmate_ID
 join H_Location on L_Location_Main.H_Location_ID=H_Location.H_Location_ID
 join L_Incarceration_Main on L_Incarceration_Main.H_Inmate_ID=H_Inmate_Main.H_Inmate_ID
 join H_Incarceration on L_Incarceration_Main.H_Incarceration_ID=H_Incarceration.H_Incarceration_ID
 join L_Counseling_Main on L_Counseling_Main.H_Inmate_ID = H_Inmate_Main.H_Inmate_ID
 join H_Counseling on L_Counseling_Main.H_Counseling_ID = H_Counseling.H_Counseling_ID
 Join S_Counseling_Days on H_Counseling.H_Counseling_ID=S_Counseling_Days.H_Counseling_ID
 where gang_type = 'STREET' and Offense = 'Sex' and Counseling_days =' TH'
```

Results | Messages

H_inmate_ID	Gang_Type	Status	H_inmate_ID	Counseling_days	Facility_Housed	Race	Name
51909	STREET	ACTIVE	51909	TH	G0	Hispanic	Jake

<u>SCRUM + Data Vault for Efficiency</u>

Using the Data Vault strategy for Data Warehouse Design allows the development teams to work more efficiently and effectively. Using a SCRUM strategy context switching is held to minimum to reduce the amount of wasted time in development. Instead of pulling teams off of current projects to aid with the creation of new modules it allows database teams to work independently. Let us take a look at this scenario: The introduction of a new referendum on criminal justice reform has required that all inmates with 2 years or more of military service who served in

Vietnam be allowed special considerations, at the current state military service is not tracked at all. In a traditional database the Data Base Administrators would have to be pulled off of their current task to aid in the creation of the new tables and how those tables fit correctly into the current structure of the database. However, using the Data Vault system one is able to evoke total quality management within the organization to prepare the table needed outside of the database structure instead of within it. This allows the DBA to stay on current task while a development team designs the new table. Since the Data Vault system is built for scalability the new table is able to be completed before removing the DBA from their current project if the need arises at all. The new table will be independent of other moving parts in the database so it can be added and will not affect the quality of data that is already in the database. Therefore, a DBA is only needed to overview and assess the situation after the the new table is linked. The DBA is not required during the planning, building, implementation, or preparation phases. This will create a more efficient environment by removing how much context switching occurs from higher level technical staff. Instead of calling off current projects, the staff is able to finish current projects and then assess new projects after completion of current projects thereby reducing wasted time.

Now using a Data Vault system that already had some of the current information available makes the process even more efficient. The data that already exist in the Data Vault can be moved to a View that allows it to be searched from the business intelligence software or through SQL Query without having to create another table. In this example, the information from the Satellite for Army was joined with information from the military hub. This will allow the end user to search only the information needed or the information can be exported to a research team.

```
Create View Army_More_Than_2 as
SELECT S_Mil_Army.Army_Location, H_Military.H_Military_ID, H_Military.Length
FROM S_MIL_Army
Inner JOIN H_Military
ON S_Mil_Army.H_Military_ID=H_Military.H_Military_ID
where length >=2
```

Figure 3.11.

Now the view can be searched for the specifications needed and saved for another time when other information from other locations might be needed.

```
Select * from Army_More_than_2
```

100 %

Results | Messages

	Army_Location	H_Military_ID	Length
1	Mayotte	52026	2
2	Vanuatu	80571	6
3	Japan	18666	7
4	El Salvador	21750	3
5	Tuvalu	95787	9
6	Thailand	59173	4
7	Sierra Leone	45382	3
8	Malaysia	01788	4
9	Azerbaijan	87442	2
10	Azerbaijan	54912	6
11	Zimbabwe	43810	6
12	Sri Lanka	35872	2
13	Peru	33386	3
14	Yemen	44535	6
15	Fiji	94534	4
16	Belgium	35564	9
17	New Zealand	07301	2
18	Nigeria	90074	4
19	Ghana	64794	6
20	Samoa	34490	2
21	Barbados	41110	9
22	Micronesia	90630	5
23	Saint Helena	32721	2
24	Uruguay	37430	3

Figure 3.12.

```
Select * from Army_More_than_2
where Army_Location = 'Vietnam'
```

100 %

Results | Messages

	Army_Location	H_Military_ID	Length
1	Vietnam	00239	4

Chapter 4: Conclusion

The primary reason for using a Data Vault structure in a correctional eco-system is to allow for agile integration of new data points based on the ever-changing missions of corrections and their inherent connection with the political structure and societal outlooks at any given point in time. The secondary reason for using a Data Vault structure in a correctional ecosystem is to increase the business intelligence to the end user. In an industry where data integrity is of utmost importance, using a Data Vault system makes perfect sense. The Data Vault structure allows for the addition of new data points without corruption or manipulation of the already established data structures inside the data warehouse. Therefore, as goals change and the need for new data is needed, data integrity of primary data is left untouched. The Data Vault structure would allow for addition of this data without corruption or manipulation of already established data structures inside the data warehouse.

The goal of this paper was to show that the Data Vault system was not only a valid method of Data Base design for the correctional industry, but a best case scenario because of the unique business correlations to business intelligence based on the one-to-one unique identification that is used in the correctional industry. The prototype that was created ran information for 100 inmates and can easily be adopted for many more. The information of only 100 inmates connected to 16 different hubs and 39 different satellites was shown to be able to create a vast collection of Big Data. The prototype created for this paper was able to be run on MS SQL Server 2012, AMD A6 Processor, and 250 GB SSD Samsung Hard Drive running 8 GB of standard RAM in a Windows 8 Environment. The business intelligence suite that produced the information from the Data Vault was the free desktop business intelligence software. Thus, the total cost of Data Vault creation and business intelligence for this prototype was no more than the cost of MS SQL Server 2012, a standard to premium laptop, and labor. This is important because in a correctional environment, like many other environments, being able to maintain efficiency cuts down on cost. As of December 2014 the cost of one bed in a correctional industry in Florida per day is $49.49 a day. This does not include special use beds which can nearly double in cost per day. The Florida DOC houses 100,873 inmates. If the cost of each bed is $49.49, it amounts to a cost of $4,992,204.77 per day (Florida Department of Corrections n.d.). What this means for a Data Vault system is allocation of bed space and tracking of the said bed space is a very important topic that should be able to be looked at by businesseintelligence models to allow for operational intelligence to successfully satisfy the operational need of a nearly 5 million dollar a day industry.

The Data Vault system allows for better business intelligence about bed management, contraband introduction, programming, and a myriad of other scalable ideas and ideologies based on the business structure and political climates that mandates organizational priority. It creates an agile system that allows for the introduction of new data without disturbing the needed data integrity of a correctional system.

In order to show this agility in an architectural sense, an SQL Query file for the entire Data Vault was created and then loaded as another separate Data Vault into MS SQL Server. This process took <2 min from start to finish. This means that structurally the Data Vault is small enough to be able to be transferred from agency to agency. This increases the efficiency as new hubs and satellites can be created specific to a certain agency and then scaled to fit other agencies that may have the same or a similar mission. This thought process would hold true in relation to small jails with only a few hundred inmates who may fall indirectly under the organizational structure of a larger state correctional agency with 20,000+ inmates or more.

In reference to the business intelligence software, depending on the amount of data requested from the MS SQL SERVER requested took between 15 min and 1 h. However, once the data was loaded into the business intelligence software the information rate had no lag whatsoever, but the initial load was fairly time-consuming. This time would however still be sufficient for small to medium operations that may not have the budgets to acquire the necessary hardware to allow the business intelligence to run in a real-time environment.

The Data Vault allows for optimal business intelligence structures based on the one- to- one identification method of the correctional industry; there is one Inmate_ID for one inmate. This creates a barrier of protection and data integrity when adding historical data or new data.

In order to protect the data integrity of the Data Vault when entering new or historical data to the Data Vault the hub The H_Inmate_Main Column H_Inmate ID has a constraint put on it that only allows unique values. This allows historical data to be entered into the Data Vault and the addition of new data into the Vault without any overlap in the unique identifier that has been set as the main business key as H_Inmate_ID.

```
CREATE UNIQUE NONCLUSTERED INDEX [UniqueID]
ON [H_Inmate_Main] (H_Inmate_ID)
```

To illustrate this process, the data was generated in the replicated Data Vault to create a mock set of historical data as inmates 00-–99 as shown below in Figure 4.1.

Figure 4.1.

```
select * from H_Inmate_Main;
select Count(H_inmate_ID) as #_INmate_ID from H_Inmate_MAin
```

100 %

Results | Messages

	Age	Gender	Education_Level	H_Inmate_ID	Security_Level	Height	Weight	Eye_Color	Name	Race
1	42	F	15	00	Med	77	164	Aquamarine	Hendrix	Native-Am
2	39	M	4	01	Med	53	321	Light SlateGray	Stanley	Black
3	42	M	9	02	Max	42	260	Aquamarine	Page	White
4	57	F	11	03	Med	49	328	Dark Violet	Tyler	Hispanic
5	65	M	14	04	Med	45	258	Thistle	Moore	Black
6	65	M	11	05	Min	52	383	PeachPuff	Reed	Asian
7	48	M	9	06	Med	51	322	Light SkyBlue	Hogan	Asian
8	64	M	14	07	Min	58	214	LightGray	Andrade	White
9	49	M	7	08	Max	43	371	Peru	Scott	Black
10	25	M	7	09	Med	51	362	LightGray	French	Native-Am
11	53	M	8	10	Med	43	318	GoldenRod	Goodman	White
12	64	F	8	11	Max	77	143	DimGrey	Levine	Asian
13	44	M	2	12	Med	75	302	Beige	Mc Cormick	Black
14	19	F	9	13	Min	49	338	Chocolate	Dominguez	Hispanic
15	47	M	11	14	Med	54	117	SlateBlue	Hobbs	Native-Am
16	38	M	7	15	Min	46	312	Dark Violet	Kemp	Hispanic
17	23	F	2	16	Max	63	356	Light SlateGray	Bell	Native-Am
18	61	F	10	17	Min	43	242	Teal	Reeves	Native-Am
19	64	M	7	18	Max	44	293	Thistle	Mckenzie	Asian
20	43	M	16	19	Med	48	289	Light SlateGrey	Costa	Native-Am
21	60	M	9	20	Med	68	231	Midnight Blue	Duran	Asian

	#_INmate_ID
1	100

When trying to alter an Inmate ID, the following exception is thrown and the statement is rejected as shown in Figure 4.2.

Figure 4.2.

```
UPDATE H_Inmate_Main
SET H_Inmate_ID='00'
WHERE H_Inmate_ID='55';
```

100 %

Messages

```
Msg 2627, Level 14, State 1, Line 1
Violation of PRIMARY KEY constraint 'XPKH_Inmate_Main'. Cannot insert duplicate key in object 'dbo.H_Inmate_Main'. The duplicate key value is (00
The statement has been terminated.
```

However, when adding new unique Inmate ID's, the system accepts the new data as shown in Figure 4.3.

Figure 4.3.

```
select * from H_Inmate_Main;
select Count(H_inmate_ID) as #_INmate_ID from H_Inmate_MAin;
```

100 %

Results | Messages

	Age	Gender	Education_Level	H_Inmate_ID	Security_Level	Height	Weight	Eye_Color	Name	Race
36	60	M	12	122	Max	NULL	239	Crimson	Eugene	Native-Am
37	42	M	16	123	Med	64	341	AntiqueWhite	Jarrett	Hispanic
38	25	M	13	124	Med	63	165	BlanchedAl...	Alejandro	Native-Am
39	54	M	12	125	Med	71	130	Ivory	Doug	White
40	31	M	11	126	Med	70	225	CadetBlue	Jered	Hispanic
41	45	M	8	127	Med	73	183	Orange	Jonah	Hispanic
42	52	F	2	128	Max	51	310	Salmon	Jess	Asian
43	64	M	4	129	Max	70	372	BlueViolet	Jody	Asian
44	19	F	9	13	Min	49	338	Chocolate	Doming...	Hispanic
45	26	M	15	130	Med	52	224	LightSlateGray	Cameron	Black
46	46	F	9	131	Med	70	106	CornflowerBl...	Armand	Asian
47	56	M	10	132	Max	70	141	LightPink	Sheldon	White
48	46	M	14	133	Med	70	206	Wheat	Jesse	Asian
49	55	M	11	134	Med	56	382	AntiqueWhite	Carlo	Hispanic
50	21	M	4	135	Med	80	255	Fuchsia	Ray	White
51	62	F	10	136	Min	69	328	DimGray	Alvin	Native-Am
52	30	M	12	137	Max	63	348	Chartreuse	Raul	Black
53	62	F	4	138	Med	76	236	DarkSlateGray	Tad	Asian
54	32	M	11	139	Med	51	125	Indigo	Taylor	White
55	47	M	11	14	Med	54	117	SlateBlue	Hobbs	Native-Am
56	49	M	12	140	Min	52	336	DimGrey	Dave	Asian

	#_INmate_ID
1	200

The simple example speaks of the ability of the Data Vault as an agile, fast, efficient, and accurate means for a correctional environment to be able to enter information with the changing socio-political climate that resides in such an industry, apart from the already proven business intelligence the Data Vault provides for a correctional system. In closing, the purpose of this paper has been appropriately met and exceeded by creating a developmental model suited for a correctional environment that is efficient and effective based on SCRUM and AGILE standards and provides efficient operational business intelligence to the end user.

References

1. Agan, A. (2011). "Sex Offender Registries: Fear Without Function?" The Journal of Law & Economics 54 (1): 207-239.
2. Casters, M., R. Bouman, and J.V. Dongen. (2010). *Pentaho Kettle Solutions Building Open Source ETL Solutions with Pentaho Data Integration*. Indianapolis, IN: Wiley.
3. Carson, A. (September 17, 2015). Prisoners in 2014. US Department of Justice, Office of Justice Programs, Bureau of Justice Statistics. http://www.bjs.gov/index.cfm?ty=pbdetail&iid=5387
4. CDCR's Strategic Offender Management System project earns national award. (n.d.) http://www.insidercdcr.ca.gov/2014/08/cdcrs-strategic-offender-management-system-project-earns-national-award/ (accessed October 15, 2016).
5. Corrections Organizational Structure. (n.d.). Michigan DOC. http://www.michigan.gov/corrections/0,4551,7-119-62761_24147--,00.html
6. Corrections Technology Association. (n.d.) Big Data and Corrections: What's the Big Issue? http://www.correctionstech.org/meeting/2013/Presentations/RR7.pdf
7. Cunningham, M.D., J.R. Sorenson, and T.J. Reidy. (2005). "An Actuarial Model for Assessment of Prison Violence Risk Among Maximum Security Inmates." Assessment, 12 (1): 40-49.
8. Database Data Warehousing Guide. (November 4, 2005). https://docs.oracle.com/cd/B19306_01/server.102/b14223/ettover.htm (accessed January 14, 2016).
9. Florida Department of Corrections. (n.d.) http://www.dc.state.fl.us/oth/Quickfacts.html (accessed February 21, 2017).
10. Foss, E. (1914). "The Ideal Prison System." *Journal of the American Institute of Criminal Law and Criminology*, 4 (5): 674-686. http://www.jstor.org/stable/1132646
11. Gnatovich, R. 2007. "Making a Case for Business Analytics." *Strategic Finance* 88. (8):46.
12. Inmon, W.H. and D. Linstedt. (2014). *Data Architecture: A Primer for the Data Scientist: Big Data, Data Warehouse and Data Vault*. San Francisco, CA: Morgan Kaufmann.
13. Inmon, W.H., D. Strauss, and G. Neushloss. (2008). *DW 2.0: The Architecture for the Next Generation of Data Warehousing*. San Francisco, CA: Morgan Kaufmann.
14. Ivan, M.L. 2014. "Characteristics of In-Memory Business Intelligence." *Informatica Economica* 18 (3): 17-25.
15. Jovanovic, V., I. Bojicic, C. Knowles, and M. Pavlic. 2012. "Persistent Staging Area Models for Data Warehouses." *Issues in Information Systems* 13 (1): 121-132.
16. Jovanovic, V., and I. Bojicic. 2012. "Conceptual Data Vault Model." http://works.bepress.com/vladan-jovanovic/9/
17. King, R.S., M. Mauer, and T. Huling. (2003). *Big Prisons, Small Towns: Prison Economics in Rural America*. Sentencing Project.

18. Linstedt, D. (2001). U.S. Patent Application No. 09/965,343.
19. Linstedt, D. (February 4, 2010). About the Data Vault. http://danlinstedt.com/allposts/datavaultcat/about-the-data-vault/
20. Linstedt, D., and K. Graziano. (2011). *Super Charge Your Data Warehouse: Invaluable Data Modeling Rules to Implement Your Data Vault.* CreateSpace.
21. Linstedt, D. and M. Olschimke. (2015). *Building a Scalable Data Warehouse with Data Vault 2.0.* San Francisco, CA: Morgan Kaufmann.
22. Iliev, A., and S. Smith. (April 2002). "Prototyping an Armored Data Vault." In International Workshop on Privacy Enhancing Technologies. Berlin Heidelberg: Springer, 144-159.
23. Marquis Electronic Offender Management Information System. (2017). http://www.marquisware.com/
24. Nichols, R. (December 2014). 2015 NASCIO Recognition Award Submission Nomination Category: Improving State Operations.
25. NIC State Statistics - California. (n.d.). http://nicic.gov/statestats/default.aspx?st=CA (accessed February 29, 2016).
26. Prisons and Politics Abstract R.A. McGee 1981.
27. Strategic Offender Management System (SOMS) CDCR. (n.d.) http://cdcr.ca.gov/SOMS/index.html (accessed February 8, 2016).
28. Sutherland, J. and J. Sutherland. (2016). *Scrum: The Art of Doing Twice the Work in Half the Time.* New York, NY: Crown Publishing.
29. Team, C.P. (2006). CMMI for Development, version 1.2.
30. What is business intelligence (BI)? (n.d.) http://searchdatamanagement.techtarget.com/definition/business-intelligence (accessed March 4, 2016).

Made in United States
North Haven, CT
05 November 2026

21772468R00063